Practical Solutions To Deal With Everyday Stress Problems

OrangeBooks Publication

1st Floor, Rajhans Arcade, Mall Road, Kohka, Bhilai, Chhattisgarh 490020

Website: **www.orangebooks.in**

© **Copyright, 2024, Author**

All rights reserved. No part of this book may be reproduced, stored in a retrieval system, or transmitted, in any form by any means, electronic, mechanical, magnetic, optical, chemical, manual, photocopying, recording or otherwise, without the prior written consent of its writer.

First Edition, 2024

PRACTICAL SOLUTIONS TO DEAL WITH EVERYDAY

STRESS PROBLEMS

SOLUTION FOR EVERYDAY STRESS

VIKAS K GARG

OrangeBooks Publication
www.orangebooks.in

About This Book

Stress and Tensions have been a crucial part of human existence, from the early days of Cavemen to Modern Corporate executives; they remain exist and haunt us. In the recent years, stress-related health problems have created devastating effects on health-related problems worldwide. Most of the stress starts when we develop the tendency to fight it rather than accept it because we always want to have an easy and prospers life without any hurdles; in fact, we all want to reach our destinations without having any sort of traffic or red light on the road which is impossible in this fast-moving and in high competition world.

I have been working in the medical field for the last 25 years. In my career I have noticed that people die and suffer in hospitals not because of various diseases, but mostly because of unmanageable stress in life. Whatever I have learned from my experience, I have included in this book.

This book is about what people, in general, expect to relieve their everyday stress without the use of any prescribed medicines. As I believe that if I have some relationship and adjustment problem with my wife, there is no medicine in this world to cure it rather than to change my attitude towards her.

I have included practical thought-changing and relaxation exercise for busy people, as it is not possible for everyone to go out for a morning walk to relax himself when he is supposed to drive 30-40 Kms. to his office and come late in the evening.

The examples, stories, and quotations are the result of a collection from various sources, such as newspapers, magazines, other speakers, and seminar participants, over the last 15 years. Unfortunately, sources were not always noted or available; hence, even though, I thankfully acknowledge the contributions to those who made my work accomplished.

How to use this book- I have carefully selected the stress-related problems according to gender and age, such as

- Men-related stress problems.
- Women-related stress problems.
- Children.
- General stress-related problems which involve everyone.

And other factors which give the stress in everyday life. This book will help you find out the exact source of stress, how to change your attitude and make harmony to day-to-day problems rather than fight them. The best way to use this book is to use it as a tool to abolish your stressful life events. I have included some diet remedies that will ease the stress-related effects on the body. These supplements are basically harmless, but do not make excessive use of them without proper guidance from your consultant.

I thank the OrangeBooks Publishing house for giving me an opportunity to write this book, and I look forward to have the cooperation in the future also.

I dedicate my book to my parents and my beloved wife; without their help and support, this endeavor would not have been fulfilled.

I hope that after using this book, you will find a positive change in your lifestyle and your stress-related matters, as I generally quote in my lectures that -

If you can't change your destiny, rather than fighting it,
Change your attitude, and the problem will be solved.

Vikas.K Garg
solutionforstress.com

Content

How To Deal With Every Day Stress Problems 1

Chapter 1 2

    What is Stress? 2

Stress Problems And Man 16

Health Problems 17

    Problem No 1 - Memory Problem Due to Regular Stressful Living 18

    Problem No 2 - Tooth Problems Due To Stress 20

    Problem No 3 - Acidity Problems Due To Stress 21

    Problem No 4 - Low Sex Drive and Poor Performance 23

    Problem No 5 - Early Andropause or male Menopause 27

    Problem No 6 - Severe Heart Burn Sansation And Uneasyness 30

    Problem No 7 - Problem Of Sleeplessness Due To Stressful Life 32

Job Related Stress 35

    Problem No 8 - Stress Caused By The Strength Of The Opponent 36

    Problem No 9 - Jobs Loss 37

    Problem No 10 - Too Much Work Related Stress 40

    Problem No 11 - Feeling Low Inspite Of Good Life 43

    Problem No 12 - Anger Managemt 46

    Problem No 13 - Stress Caused By Fear Of Failing 52

    Problem No 14 - Stress Caused By Having Excessive Helpful Nature. As People Around Misuse It And Puts Extra Burden On My Life 54

    Problem No 15 - Unforgivness 57

Stress Caused By Personal And Family Problems 59

    Problem No 16 - Financial Problems 60

    Problem No 17 - Relationship Problems 63

    Problem No 18 – Smoking Cigarette 67

    Problem No 19 - Excess Drinking 69

Ladies Oriented Stress Problems 72

Health Problems Due To Stress 72

Problem No 20 - Depressions Due To The Extreme Stress 73

Problem No 21 - Menstrual Problems 78

Problem No 22 - Pregnancy Related Problems 83

Problem No 23 - Early Mother Hood Related Problems 85

Problem No 24 - Menopause Stage Related Stress 87

Problem No 25 - Headaches Due To Stress 90

Problem No 26 - Starve To Stress - Slim Forever 95

Problem No 27 - Skin Problems Due To Stress 98

Problem No 28 - Nails Problems Due To Stressful Life 101

Emotional Problems Due To Stress 103

Problem No 29 - Negative Thoughts 104

Problem No 30 - Eating Problems Related To Stress 107

Problem No 31 - Worrying Too Much 111

Problem No 32 - Adjustment Disorder 114

Problem No 33 - Self harming Attitude 117

Problem No 34 - How To Make Balance Between Home And Office 120

Problem No 35 - Behavior Related Stress By Your Boss 123

Problem No 36 - Stress Due To The Colleges In The Office 125

Old Age Related Stress And Relationships Problems 127

Problem No 37 - Old Age Related Health Problems Which Can Increase Stress 128

Child Stress Related Problems 131

Problem No 38 - When Your Child Is Depressed 132

Problem No 39 - Exam Related Stress Problems 136

Problem No 40 - Child Obesity And Eating Habits 139

Problem No 41 - Teen Behavior Related Problems 142

Problem No 42 - Concentration On Studies 149

Problem No 43 - Poor Time Management Leads To Stress 153

Problem No 44 - Vacation Related Stress 156

Problem No 45 - Traffic Jams Stress 159

Problem No 46 - Dealing With Road Rage 161

Problem No 47 - Car Break down stress 163

Problem No 48 - Seasonal Affective Stress Problems 164

Problem No 49 - Stress In The BPO Sector 166

Problem No 50 - Mobile Lost Stress 170

How To Deal With Every Day Stress Problems

Stress – The most common word we hear nowadays than ever before. The rapid growth of modernization and the lust to earn more has made this word a permanent place in our daily talk.

From wall street to tokyo stock exchange, the high profile executives are the worst affected by this epidemic. In modern times, stress has become a buzzword and legitimate concern for people of all walks of life. No one is immune to stress. Straight from birth until death, an individual is exposed to various types of stress. Stress is such a field that can never be avoided.

It is a general concept that Stress is the one of the worst enemy of the mankind, but this is not true. In fact, the **unmanaged stress** is the worst enemy, as it is the lead cause of over 70% of all hospitalizations around the world. The main cause is that we push our bodies to the extreme limits without taking a break for ourselves.

If we go for the medical definitions for stress, it says –

Stress can be defined as our Mental, Physical, and Emotional reactions to any demands or threats.

To understand these definitions better, let's take an example: Suppose a person drops a pen from his hands while standing in his office. He would certainly pick it up as expected, but he is suffering from severe backache, then this very simple work would become a highly stressful thing for him. We can see that from morning to evening, we perform hundreds of actions from our bodies and face different types of emotions and stress naturally. Therefore, life without Stress is impossible, but life without the effects of STRESS is easy. Or in other words, let us take STRESS as the Spice flavor in our daily routine life; if it is too much, the food will certainly be hard to eat and if it is too little, it will became tasteless. Therefore, the Stress Management not only teaches us how to eat properly but also to make our food tasteful and beneficial in spite of its bad taste.

This book discusses the key issues related to 50 common things of our daily routine that create unnecessary STRESS and – its causes, its effects on the body as being a Man-Woman-Child and Behavior related treatment, several unconventional treatments including Practical exercises, Diet related assistance and Self Motivational Exercises are added. In fact, it teaches the method to control Unmanaged Stress and live a long and healthy life.

Chapter 1

What is Stress?

The word Stress is derived from the Latin word **"Stringere"**. Stress was popularly used in the seventeenth century to mean hardship, strain, adversity or Affliction. It was used in the eighteenth and nineteenth centuries to denote force, pressure, strain or strong efforts with reference to an object or person. A Stress acts as a force on body to produce strain. It is an adaptive response to a situation that is challenging to a person.

<u>**The concept of Stress**</u> – It was first introduced in Life sciences by Hans Selye in 1936. There are different views of different people on the basis of their personal experiences, like for some businessmen, it is a frustration or emotional tension, some suggest that it is a physical or mental pressure; these restrict and act as a hindrance in the performance of an individual. It is pressure people feel in life due to their reaction to a situation. **Hans Selye** defines stress as an **"adaptive response to the external situation that results in physical, psychological or behavioral deviation for organizational participants."**

But this is only one side of the coin; on the other side, there is always a constrictive and positive side. Side A which shows the ill effects of Stress as Distress, the other side present the U-Stress or the utility Stress. We will discuss in our next chapter regarding the types of stress, and how they can be more productive in our daily lives.

The Concept Of Mind

We all know about the effects of Stress nowadays. Every health article around the world has discussed the effects on our everyday lives, but in spite of all the knowledge we gain, our daily routine remains the same - Stressful as ever before. Why is it so? Why do we feel miserable and helpless about minor losses we have or lose all sorts of intelligence or wisdom by slight of provocations by others? We all read a lot about the accidents of Road Rage, which involves socialized people of the cities, yet they behave like professional criminals on the roads. We keep thinking about lots of foolish negative things about ourselves, yet we know that god has gifted much better status than most of the people.

The answer lies in our concept of mind. Our mind consists of 3 major parts in general.

THE CONSCIOUS MIND (10%)

It is the thin slice of the mind with the unconscious forming. The greater part of the mind is like an iceberg, with the greater part existing below the surface of awareness. It is a state of doing actions such as Running, Eating, Thinking, etc.

THE UNCONSCIOUS MIND - (90%)

This part of the mind stores up all the experiences, memories and motivations that are out of awareness. This part influences the Behavior to a great extent. It is the most powerful part of the mind and stores 90% of habits. Past Experiences are stored in it, which helps us to judge our all performances according to our past experiences. For example, a child would never put his hand on a burning candle fire, if he had burnt his hand before. The previous experiment would quickly recall him the same results if he dares to do the same thing again.

SUBCONSCIOUS MIND

It is like valve that allows memories from the unconscious mind to emerge to conscious mind via dreams, etc. It consists of sleeping stage: The process of dreaming happens in the territory of subconscious mind.

This whole concept can be easily understood by the Diagram below, which clearly indicates all parts of the mind. It represents the Sad and Happy parts of the mind, which are applicable to all of us, but there may be some variations according to the atmosphere and the family concept, which makes the happy part much bigger than other people around us.

The Sad and happy parts of the Mind

We have basically three parts of the mind, described above; besides this, in the Unconscious Mind, there are two different parts which represent the **Sad and the Happy memories** of our entire lives. We still do not know why the Sad Part is bigger than the happy part in the mind, but there is one example in this, which clarifies the above statement:-

DIAGRAM

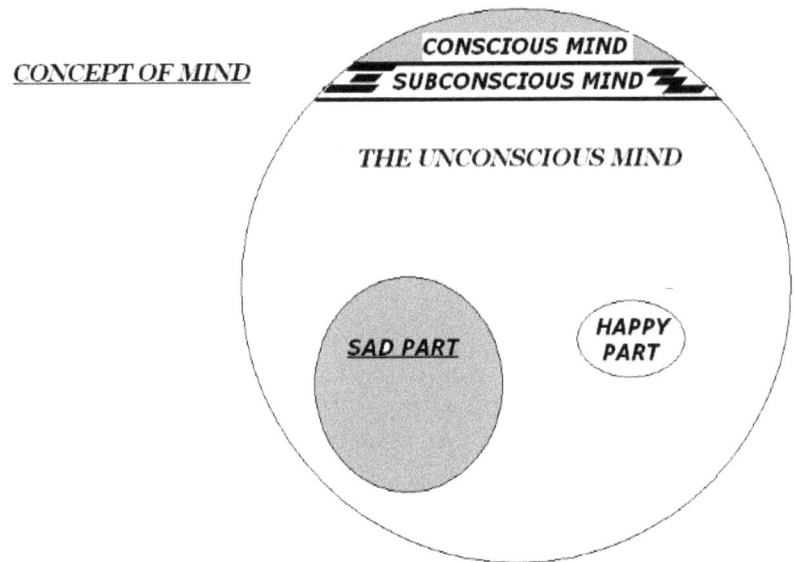

Example - A

Imagine a newly born child of around 10-15 days lying in his cradle alone. He gets the urge to have milk or any other thing, and there is no one around at that moment. Now, the question arises: What efforts would he make to get what he wants?

Certainly, the answer would be in the form of crying at his full abilities, which summons his mother to get his demands fulfill.

By crying or diverting his mind to the sad part, the child will make his mind in the framework of the negative side. Now, for each and every requirements, his mind quickly adopts the same framework of using the negative sad part.

When he goes to school, he always gets vacations or excuses for not doing his homework by falsely claiming health problems or any ill-happenings in his family. This imagination of solving his problems dominates his entire personality and his ability to handle the Stress in his whole life. As the child grows up, he uses this pattern of negativity every time he finds himself under stress, and these negative feelings become part of his character. We all possess this problems, but there is only one difference between our personalities - the way we all have grown-ups; some are born rich and face few difficulties in their lives, and others may not be so lucky to have such luck. To further clarify the above statement, let us have one more practical Exercise.

Practical Exercise -1

Close your eyes for five minutes and try to remember some of the most difficult and painful days of your life. Try to remember them as much as you can and make a virtual list of each bad day.

Next Step: Try to remember some of the most joyful and happy days of your life within the same framework. After doing this exercise, you will be surprised to see that compared to the sad days, it is very hard to remember happy days in our lives. The main reason behind this example is to justify the concept of mind, which is dominated by the sad aspects of life in general. In practice, if we calculate our daily routine, for example –

- My Daughter Is Not Answering My Phone Call.
- My Son Is Not Back Home After His Classes.
- My Wife Is Not Talking Properly To Me Today.
- I Received A Miss Call On My Cell In The Middle Of The Night.

There are several examples which happen every day, which increase our stress levels without reviewing the real facts. In the context of the above situations, there may be other reasons behind them.

- My Daughter Was Busy With Her Friends At The Canteen, And She Kept Her Mobile In Her Bag. Therefore, She Did Not Attend My Call.
- My Son Was Busy Taking Notes For His Studies, It Is Much More Important For Him Than Informing Me, That Is Why He Is Late.

- My Wife Is Having Some Menstrual Pain, Which Gives Her Restless Sleep At Night, Which She Does Not Want To Share With Me.
- It May Be Some Wrong Telephone Number From The Other End, Thanks To Long International Telephonic Codes.

This is only a glimpse of the examples of the concept we have in our minds, which quickly follow the sad part of our mind. Imagine if all the four examples happened to us; we would simply have a lot of bad or negative thoughts about the situations and create a lot of stress for ourselves as well as for others in our family. Practically, if you find, life in today's world is far safer than we think. We have got all sorts of facilities and the fastest mode of communication than our ancestors. Believe it or not, in the year 1899, the **British Science Academy** declared that "In the last days of the century, all sorts of inventions and explorations have been invented, and there is no hope for anything new in the coming century". In just 100 years, we have all sorts of good things in our daily lives, but we still tend to be more stress-prone than ever before.

On a typical day in the brain, trillions of messages are sent and received. The messages that are happy and upbeat are carried by the brain's "HAPPY MESSENGERS" (technically known as Biogenic Amine/Endorphin System). Other messages are somber and quiet. They are carried by the brain's "SAD MESSENGERS".

Most nerve centers receive input from both types of messengers. As long as this input is balanced, everything runs along on an even keel. Stress, however, causes problems with the brain's Happy Messengers. When life is smooth, the happy messages keep up with demand. But when too much stress is placed on the brain, the Happy Messengers begin to fall behind on their deliveries. As the stress continues, the happy messages begin to fail. Important nerve centers then receive mostly SAD MESSAGES, and the brain becomes distressed. The person enters a state of brain chemical imbalance known as - OVERSTRESS. OVERSTRESS makes people feel terrible. With SAD MESSAGES overwhelming the happy messages, a person feels "overwhelmed" by life. People complain of being tired, unable to fall asleep or to obtain a restful night's sleep. They have plagues of aches and pains, lack of energy, and lack of enjoyment of life. They feel depressed, anxious, or just unable to cope with life.

You must have noticed many times that in spite of having so many luxuries and facilities in our lives we are getting more and more stressed and irritated than before. In practice, we should be more polite and relaxed with the help of the remote control of almost everything in our lives. I personally believe that the problem lies deep inside our attitude. Let's take an example we all do every day-

Suppose Mr. **A** is stressed in the morning because of his professional problems. He shout at his Wife and stresses her in the morning; he again shouts and stresses at his driver on the way to his office; at the office, he again follows the same temperament by shouting at his joiner staff. He is still stressed, but he has created a lot of people around him who are deeply irritated and stressed by his behavior.

If we notice all these people who have been stressed by Mr. A, they would eventually release their anger on other people, for instance-

- His wife releases her anger on the housemaid - who takes this problem to her family and releases her anger on her husband and children.

- His driver gets irritated and shouts at fellow drivers on the way.

- His staff releases their anger on the customers or their fellow workers.

So at last, there is a series of stressed people, who are creations of a single fellow named Mr. A. If Mr. A would have absorbed his problems and remained cool, there would not be any problem for anyone.

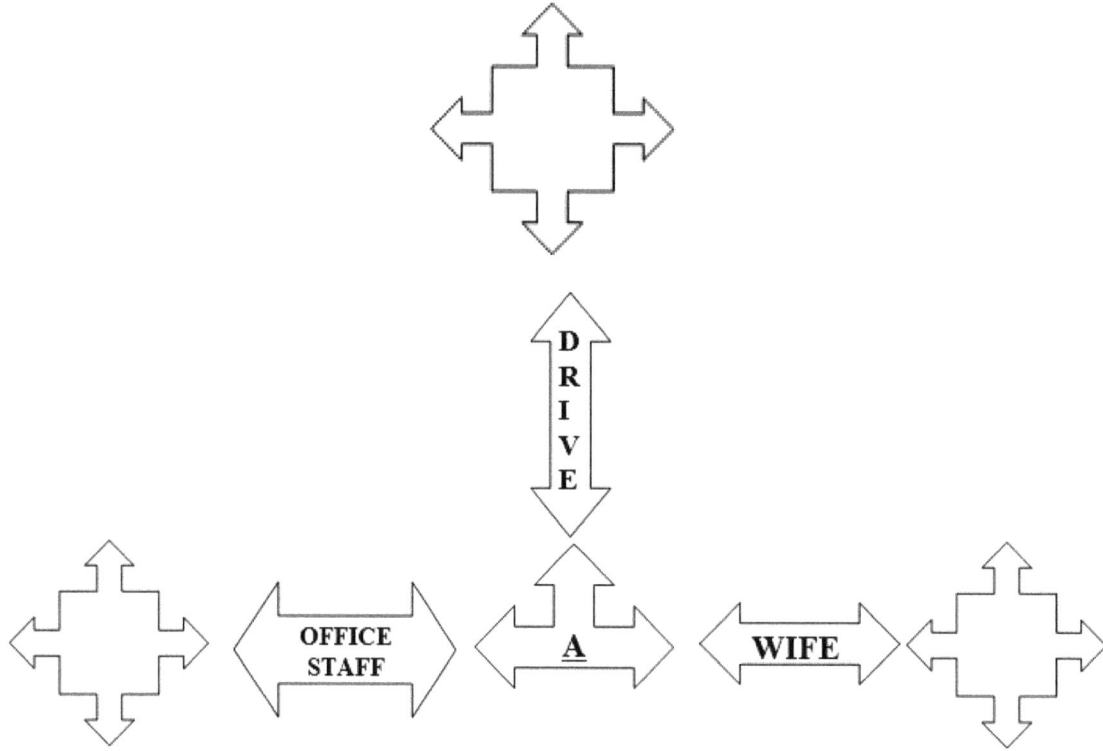

(B) FIGHT OR FLIGHT, FREEZZE RESPONSE

When pressures seem threatening more than we can handle, our bodies react quickly to supply protection by "turning on the juices" and preparing to take action. This reaction is known as the "**fight or flight**" response. Imagine, while going on a vacation to a remote area, we face a threatening tiger; for instance, we quickly make up our mind for two choices: either to fight the tiger or to run away.

While searching for actions, our body prepares quickly to respond. The heart begins to race, breathing rate increases, muscles become tense, and mind processes information rapidly.

This natural response to danger helps us from the age of cavemen to protect and to survive.

Now, we take another **Example** from our everyday lives.

Just imagine you are going out for a Party with your wife at night. Suddenly, a cycle rider comes from nowhere and you halt on the brake of your car. You may come out of your car and probably slap him for his foolish action, which could have created an accident. This action is a clear example of **Fight** because your mind has clearly indicated you about your supremacy over the cycle rider.

Now, another course of action -

You are coming back from the same party, and on another road, a large SUV just overtakes you, and you hardly control your car. From the other SUV come down 4 to 5 young boys, badly drunk and ready for a brawl on the street. In spite of your anger, you quickly think of escaping this situation either by saying sorry to those boys because your action will certainly put you as well as your wife's safety in question. This is a perfect example of **Flight**, as your mind has given you a clear message of your weakness in the current situation.

I believe I have cleared the concept of **FIGHT OR FLIGHT RESPONSE.**

FREEZE RESPONSE

You may have seen several cases when a person just gets frozen like a dummy in etremely stressful situation where his mind cannot judge the action or simply what to do.

Medical Aspect of Stress

Stress Hormone Cortisol

Cortisol is a hormone produced by your adrenal glands. It falls into a category of hormones known as *"glucocorticoids",* referring to their ability to increase blood glucose levels.

What does Cortisol do...?

Cortisol is part of the <u>fight or flight response</u>. Faced with a "life or death" situation, Cortisol increases the flow of glucose (as well as protein and fat) out of your tissues and into the bloodstream in order to increase energy and physical readiness to handle the stressful situation or threat.

Three Happy Messengers in our Mind

Nature has also provided us with the three Happy Messengers: **SEROTONIN, NORADRENALIN**, and **DOPAMINE**. These are the brain chemicals that begin to malfunction when stress levels become more than a person can handle, and they also provide the satisfaction and enjoyment in the life in daily basis.

- **Serotonin**

Serotonin lets you sleep

The Happy Messenger, Serotonin, must work properly in order for you to sleep well. Serotonin is responsible for making sure that your body's physiology is set for sleeping. If Serotonin does not do its job properly, you will not be able to obtain a restful sleep, no matter how hard you try.

Serotonin Sets Your Body Clock

Inside every one of our brains is a very accurate "Clock". This time-keeping equipment functions like the composer of a symphony orchestra. Just as the player of the orchestra keeps all the various instruments playing in rhythm, the Body Clock keeps all the various functions of your body coordinated and moving to the same rhythm. The Body Clock is located deep in the center of the brain, in a little group of cells known as the Pineal Gland. Within the Pineal Gland is a store-house of the messenger Serotonin, which is the chemical "mainspring" of the Clock.

Each day, the Serotonin is chemically converted to a related compound, Melatonin, and then the Melatonin is converted right back to Serotonin. The whole cycle from Serotonin to Melatonin and back to Serotonin takes exactly 25 hours, forming your Body's Clock. Our bodies produce melatonin in the bean-size pineal gland nestled deep inside our brains; it is also produced in the retinas of our eyes. Melatonin production is stimulated by darkness and shuts down in the presence of bright light (especially sunlight). Normally, the pineal gland starts increasing its melatonin production around 9 P.M. Hormone levels peak between 2 A.M. and 4 A.M. and then return to their normal time levels.

The body clock and the body temperature

Every 24 hours, your body temperature cycles from high to low, varying by as much as one degree. When it is time to wake up and be active, your body temperature rises slightly. When it is time to fall asleep, your body temperature dips slightly. Most of us have felt how difficult it is to fall asleep on a very warm night when you toss and turn and wish you could cool off. Contrast this with the relative comfort when one is tucked in a nice bed in a room that is slightly cool or even downright cold. To achieve the best sleep, the body thermostat is supposed to lower slightly at night, a timing which is coordinated by your Body Clock.

Body Clock and the stress-fighting hormones in the body

The body has a vital hormone called Cortisol, which is the body's chief stress-fighting hormone. When Cortisol secretion is high, the body shifts to a "war footing". It is prepared for stress conditions. Cortisol drops substantially in the evening as one relaxes, settles down, and prepares for sleep. As with body temperature, the ups and downs of your stress-fighting hormone must cycle correctly during a 24-hour day for you to achieve a relaxing night's sleep and wake refreshed. Any disturbance of your Cortisol cycle and restful sleep will become very difficult.

Body clock and the sleep cycles

After falling asleep, one normally goes DEEPER and DEEPER into sleep, finally reaching a state of deep, soothing sleep. Then sleep becomes LIGHTER and LIGHTER until one enters dreaming sleep. Then, the whole cycle begins over again. About every 90 minutes, one goes through this cycle. In the early evening, the cycle pauses for a relatively long time in the deepest restorative phase. As the evening progresses, the amount of time spent in deep restorative sleep lessens, and one spends more and more time dreaming. In order for one to feel rested, this sleep pattern must be cycling properly. And, of course, the cycle is regulated by your internal Body Clock.

Stress affects the sleep pattern

The Body Clock is essential for the proper harmony of your body temperature, stress-fighting hormone, and sleep cycles. In order to fall asleep easily, sleep soundly and awake refreshed, your Body Clock must be functioning properly. The Happy Messenger, Serotonin, is the "mainspring" of the Body Clock. If stress causes Serotonin to fail, the Body Clock will stop working. You will not be able to obtain a restful sleep, no matter how hard you try.

Since Serotonin Is Usually The First Happy Messenger To Fail Under Stress, The First Sign Of Overstress Will Usually Be The Inability To Obtain Restful Sleep.

- **Noradrenalin:**

Energy Provider to the Body

When you are frightened, Adrenalin is released into your bloodstream by your adrenal glands. You are ready for "fight or flight". Another type of Adrenalin, named Noradrenalin, is one of the Happy Messengers. Noradrenalin has many important functions in the body's nervous system. The one that most concerns us here, however, is the role of Noradrenalin in setting your energy levels. Proper performance of Noradrenalin in the brain is important for you to feel energized. Without enough brain Noradrenalin, you feel exhausted, tired, and without energy. People with Noradrenalin failure become ever more fatigued. They do not seem to have any energy to do anything. Running your brain with low Noradrenalin is of the same kind as running your car with a fading battery. Sooner or later, it just won't start.

- **Dopamine:**

The Pleasure and Pain regulator

This is the most important Happy Hormone in the body, known as the Dopamine. It is found in our body's naturally happening machinery for regulating pain. It is likely that a certain baseline secretion of Endorphin occurs at all times in the body.

This Happy Messenger, Dopamine, seems to be concentrated in areas of the brain immediately adjacent to where the major Endorphin-releasing mechanisms lie. When Dopamine function declines, Endorphin function also declines. Hence, when too much stress causes failure of Dopamine function, it also causes loss of your body's natural "pain killer".

Dopamine also runs your body's "Pleasure Centre". This is the area of your brain that allows you to enjoy life. When stress interferes with your Dopamine function, the Pleasure Center becomes inoperative. Normally, pleasure activities no longer give any pleasure. With severe Dopamine/Endorphin malfunction, life becomes painful and devoid of any pleasure.

Example- Suppose a Man loves Pizza at dinner; today, he is in a very happy mood and loves his pizza till the last bite. Next day, he has a terrible day, a fight with his wife... later with his colleague in office, again, he goes for pizza at dinner in restaurant; same pizza tastes horrible, even he can't eat a full on this day. Now, the problem is not in the Pizza, but the problem is in his mind deep inside, where all Happy Hormones are blown.

Why Do We "Stress Out"?

Essentially, we stress out for two main reasons...

We *perceive* a situation as dangerous, difficult, or painful.

Our Perceptions = How Stressed We Feel

We often identify specific events, people, or situations that seem to make us feel stressed. In reality, it's only **WE** who decide to feel stressed or not stressed about it.

The interesting thing about stress is that it begins with our own perceptions of things!

Types of stress

There is a great misconception about stress that we very much believe that it is the same thing in general-painful, a Disaster for health, but it is not true. Stress can be divided into four different categories according to its effects and characteristics.

Types of STRESS- We face every day

Experiencing some amount of stress in our lives is protective and adaptive. Our responses to Stress help our minds and bodies to prepare for difficult challenges and to react appropriately in a time of crisis. In fact, a certain amount of stress is necessary to help us perform at our best. Stress adds flavor, challenge and opportunity to life. Without stress, life could become quite dull and unexciting.

There are four types of Stress.

1. *Distress* is a continuous experience of feeling overwhelmed and behind in our responsibilities. It is the sense of being imposed upon by difficulties with no light at the end of the tunnel. Examples include financial difficulties, conflicts in relationships, managing a chronic illness, or experiencing trauma. High amount of Distress leads us to a stage called **Burnout.** This is a stage when our bodies run out of the energy, and we are totally exhausted.

2. *Rust out*- When the task is not up to the mark of person's ability, it presents the Rust out phase of stress, because of its Boredom and unchallenging nature. Now, let's take a simple example of Stress in everyday life that reflects this classification.

We take two teachers from different classes -

- A science teacher from High school named Mr. A
- Another Science teacher from primary school named Mr. B

Both are satisfied in their job and have mild stress in their lives.

Suppose if we ask them to change their classes for teaching, what will happen?

Mr. A feels ultimate boredom and usefulness of his capabilities due to the lower level of his job. In spite of the good salary, he feels that he is wasting his talents and energy, which is of no use.

Mr. B will ultimately find his way tough and difficult because he will be unable to teach the high school class. He will try to defend himself to his full abilities in order to deal with high school students, and eventually, his total energy will be exhausted and he will be in the Burnout stage of Stress. If we double the salary of Mr. B, he will not be ready to teach the class.

In both ways, A and B are under high stress because of their job profiles. Even their prospectives for Stress are different -

Mr. A Is under the influence of Rust out Phase of Stress.

Mr. B is under the influence of Distress Phase of Stress.

And ultimately, both of them will quit their jobs.

3. _Eustress-_ is the other form of stress that is positive and beneficial. We may feel challenged, but the sources of the stress are opportunities that are meaningful to us. Eustress helps provide us with energy and motivation to meet our responsibilities and achieve our goals. Examples include graduating from college, getting married, receiving a promotion, or changing jobs. This is a state of mind which is full of joy and happiness, without having a feelings of fatigue or negative feelings, which can disturb the status of mind. It can be resembled with a person on a world tour with his loved one. Despite a long journey and climate change, he will try to enjoy himself to his full abilities.

I remember a perfect example of a great business Tycoon named Earl P. Haney, who was suffering from stomach ulcers in his early 20s. His conditions became from bad to worse up to such an extent that he lost his body weight from 175 pounds to 90 pounds. He became so ill that at that time, the specialist declared that his case was incurable. He suffered all sorts of pains in his hospital bed. At that stage, he imagined that he would not going to survive a long time, and before dying he wanted to go around the world, being a wealthy person; all the suitable arrangements were made for his long travel plans. He also arranged for a casket and all the medical help required. Everyone believed that he would not be coming back due to his extremely poor conditions.

As I said earlier, the positive effects of the Eustress are magnificent in all aspects. Within the days of Earl P. Haney's sea voyage, he recovered rapidly from his conditions. He enjoyed all sorts of foods available, which would have been highly forbidden for him if his doctors had come to know. He enjoyed his life to the fullest and finally came back after covering the whole world and lived a long life thereafter.

4. _Imaginary Stress-_ You will be surprised to know that the imaginary Stress is as dangerous as the real one. In this, the Mind constantly revolves around certain Problems. Even if the person looks normal from outside, this can affect his mental as well as physical performance in a long run.

This type of Stress is the most common type we face regularly. Imagine, we keep thinking about a certain problem throughout the night, and the next morning, when we face the problem with having the possible way to tackle it, almost most of the time, I have seen that a new and easier way to that problem is already existed, and we make our minds so confused that we overlook that easier and peaceful way.

I can say that it is because the one who is the greatest master of all of us, God always takes care of us, whether we always ignore his existence in the middle of troubles. It is a strange example that during the Second World War, heart disease killed almost two million civilians due to their imaginary war-related problems and worries.

This whole concept can be more easily understood by the chart below. It clearly represents the performance capability of any person, either me or you. We all face the same consequences as the stress level increases or decreases in our daily affairs. This chart is known as the **Stress Tolerance Chart**. It represents our ability graph by the 0-100 markings. 0 is the lowest, and 100 is the highest number we can give to our abilities to cope with any stressful situations. This is followed by the situation which is called the rust-out stage of stress.

Stress Tolerance Chart

This Chart is a guide to evaluating the effects of Stress on ourselves. The higher the figure, the more its effects on the human body. We consider that the average human can face the ultimate of 100 (in numbers) of stress on his body.

DIAGRAM

According to Dr. T.H.holmes and Dr. R.H.Rahe (**journal of Psychomatic Research No-11, 1967**), specific events are weighed on a scale from 0-100 according to their effects on the health of any person. Some of the major Stress in the life are -

Events	Life Change Units
Death of a spouse	100
Divorce	73
Marital Separations	65
Imprisonments	63
Death of a close relative	63
Personal injury or illness	53
Marriage/engagements	50
Winning a lottery	50
Loss of job	47
Marital reconciliation	45
Retirements	45
Illness in the family	44

Pregnancy	44
Sexual problems	39
Birth of a child	39
Business readjustments	39
Change in financial state	38
Death of close friend	37
Change to different work	36
Repayment of loan	31
Change of job	29
Son /daughter leaving home	29
Beginning/end of school, college	26
Change in living conditions	25
Change in personal habits	24
Trouble with the boss	23
Moving house	20
Change of school/college	20
Change of sleeping habits	16
Holidays	13

Burnout stage of Stress

The Burnout stage can be defined as a stage of mental and physical exhaustion caused by excessive and prolonged Stress. There are three stages of Burnout, which includes-

1. Stress Arousal

It includes symptoms of Irritability, Anxiety, Bruxism (grinding teeth at night), insomnia, forgetfulness and regular Headaches.

2. Energy Conservation

It includes symptoms of lateness at work, decreased sexual desires, Social withdrawal and increased dependencies like smoking, drinking, etc.

3. Exhaustions

In this, the symptoms are- chronic Depression/sadness, regular Mental and physical fatigue, desire to move away from society or the worst, to commit suicide.

These stages usually occur from stage 1 to stage 3. Even though the process can be stopped at any point, depending upon the events which lead to this stage.

Effects of Unmanageable Stress on the human body.

As far as the effects of stress on human body are concerned, it can be a major cause of hospitalization, around 70% in total, in the world because we tend to overlook any initial signal of stress-related disorders by painkillers and other OTC (Over The Counter) medicines as they are freely available worldwide. The effects on the human body related to stress can be to such an extent that it can not be included in this little book. Moreover, we are discussing the remedies for our daily stress problems, but still, I am including some basic facts and effects, which indicate a glimpse of these effects.

Body Organs	Normal	Under Tension	Acute pressure	Chronic pressure (stress)
Brain	Blood supply normal	Blood supply up	Thinks more clearly	Headaches or migraines
Feelings	Happy	Serious	Increased concentration	Anxiety, Irritations
Mouth	Normal	Reduced	Reduced	Dry mouth, Grinding Teeth at night
Muscles	Blood supply normal	Blood supply up	Improved performance and Tolerance	Muscular fatigue pain and swelling
Heart	Normal blood pressure	Increased rate and blood pressure	Improved performance	Hypertension and chest pains
Lungs	Normal	Increased respiration rate	Improved performance	Regular Coughs and asthma
Stomach	Normal	Reduced blood supply and increased acid secretion	Reduced blood supply reduces digestion	Acidity, Constipations and Ulcers
Bowels	Normal blood supply and bowel activity	Reduced blood supply and increased bowel activity	Reduced blood supply reduces digestion	Abdominal pain and diarrhea
Sexual Organs	Male-normal	Lack of interest and poor performance	Decreased blood supply	Impotence
Sexual Organs	Female-normal periods etc	Irregular periods	Decreased blood supply	Menstrual and Gyne. disorders
Skin	Healthy	Excess Oily /Dry skin	Decreased blood supply	Acnes/Dryness and rashes
Sleep cycle	Healthy on Time	Slightly Disturbed	Body Clock Malfunction/poor sleep pattern	Chronic insomnia

I am closing this chapter with the famous words of Dr. Alexis Carrel:

Those Who Do Not Know How To Fight Their Worries Die Very Young.

Stress Problems And Man

Men have more public and professional life as compared to women around the world. Due to the supremacy part of society, men have been bestowed with the ego since the birth of this society. In order to prove their dominance, men have always ignored health problems and consist an ego which prevents them from expressing their feelings to anyone. Men have the worst health and longevity statistics as compared to women; due to man stress, he is more prone to have dependencies profile, which includes - drinking, smoking, use of drugs and other stimulants which not only shorten their life span but also create problems in the society.

It is really ironic that in the whole world, the man dies much shortly before woman. The main reason behind this is the poor attitude of health awareness, tendency to take unnecessary risks and poor diet - all these are related to the excess stress, which vacuums up to the mind, and because of this, man tends to die an early death.

Here, we are discussing some of the most stress-creating problems faced by the men around the world.

Stress is the wear and tear the body experiences as people adjust to the ever-changing environment. It is relative to every individual. What may be considered as stressful to one person may not be true to another. Since stress factors are part of daily life, the goal is not to eliminate stress but to find the optimal level where the stress factors motivate the individual to continue his/her life and not be overwhelmed. This is called stress management.

Life without these stress factors may lead to boredom, dejection and depression. On the other hand, the excess of stress can cause serious effects on the body. Unfortunately, Men around the world are careless and do not consider their health, until something goes wrong with their bodies. Here, in this section, I have concluded some of the most stressful events that give stress to anyone on the day-to-day living. The list has been included with daily stress related to Health, Jobs, Emotions, family and Finances, and lastly, dependencies-related stress problems. Unfortunately, India is one of the most unhappy countries in the world, ranking 126 out of 136 in total, because we deal with the worst way of managing Stress.

With the experiences of dealing with practical solutions, I have included all the easy and adoptable solutions for these problems as I am very much aware that it is not sensible to ask anyone to go for Yoga or Morning Walks on the regular basis. While giving the workshops in the corporate Companies, I always provide the audiences with the most adoptable solutions that can be used even at the office premises whenever anyone feels stressed.

Health Problems

›Vikas K Garg

Problem No 1 - Memory Problem Due to Regular Stressful Living

Stress Builder -
I Have Developed A Very Poor Memory Nowadays

Explanation- People who are often stressed out are far more likely to develop memory problems than other people. A study conducted in Rush University Medical study by Dr. Robert Wilson suggests that those people who most often are anxious or depressed are more likely to have 40 times more chances of memory loss as compared to a normal person. Not only have these persons lost their cognition, but they show many changes in their brains that are associated with Alzheimer's disease. People with mild cogitative impairment have some trouble remembering things, but they do not have any other significant disabilities. Not all people develop Alzheimer's disease, a much more serious disease, but about 10% to 15% of people can do it. Dr. Robert Wilson analyzed data from two large studies involving around 1256 people, and participants were rated on how prone they were to worry and depression. The latest research suggests that chronic stress may harm parts of the brain responsible for responding to the stress- an area that is also associated with memory functioning. So, it is a real fact that the more you worry, the more you make your mind forgetful, which can lead to a deadly disease.

Another study was conducted on rodents at university of California found that instead of Cortisol, Corticotrophin release hormone (**CRH**) plays a vital role in blocking memory after stressful periods.

Stress is always a compounding factor in modern lifestyle. While stress has been implicated in the development of lifestyle diseases like diabetes and heart disease, its effects

Was largely unknown, but the recent studies show that constant stress can create memory problems in people who constantly remain stressed.

Supportive plans to combat this stress-

I have dedicated this whole book on practical and easy remedies for every known stress-related problems. In the coming pages, you will come to know different methods to deal with stress. Here, I am describing some of the time-tested methods for memory improvement, which will sharpen the memory as we grow older.

1. In your free time, try to join a conference or seminar on a topic you are not familiar with or indulge in any hobby like swimming, tennis or anything physical that you always wanted to do; you will feel the difference in your life.

2. Try to remember the things you always wanted to do or develop as a new interest in life; it not only gives you a sense of achievments but also makes you happier inside.
3. If it is possible, try to do mathamathical games in your spare time. Nowadays, you can install memory games app on your mobile. It will also affect the white matter in your brain, which is deemed necessary to maintain good memory.
4. Try to use the other hand, like if you are right-handed, try to use your left hand to do the regular job, like brushing your teeth, etc. This would activate the other part of your mind, which is quite unfamilier with doing regular jobs. This would enhance the memory in long run.

As we grow older, we tend to believe that we have learnt a lot in our lives, but after a significant age, if we develop any new hobby, it will not only relese our stress but also sharpen the mind, and we will become less forgetful in daily affairs.

There is an old saying which is perfect for our attitude -

***By the time we know and perfect ourselves to play the rules of the game,
We are too old to play it.***

Problem No 2 - Tooth Problems Due To Stress

Stress Builder- I have developed teeth problems, although I always brush twice

Explanations- Whether you believe it or not, but most of the tooth-related problems start with your emotional imbalance. Worry can even cause tooth decay. Unpleasant emotions, such as those caused by worry and fear, can upset the body's calcium balance and cause tooth decay. One more type of problem, sensitivity problems of teeth, is also a gift of chronic stress; as I have said earlier, the unconscious mind stores all our good and bad memories after they happen in our daily routine. If we have a very stressful day, and inspite of our best effort, we cannot justify ourselves in front of our Boss or any other person, at night, the same feeling of expression conquers our mind, and we begin to start grinding our teeth (Medically it is called Burixm), which not only destroys the enamel coating but also leads to tooth decay.

Supportive plans to combat this stress-

It is not possible to fight for our rights every time we face stressful situations. In today's complex world, we know very well that it is impossible to sustain a job anywhere without facing humiliating situations. The best remedy for facing these situations are-

- Rather than coming directly to home, try to spend at least 15 minutes in fresh air in the nearby garden. It will help you to forget the office problems, and you will be more relaxed.
- Now, Teeth Guard is available in the market; it works like a barrier between the upper and lower teeth, and you can use it as a precaution to prevent further damage.
- If the negativity is related to a particular person overwhelming you, try to analyze the source of that problem. It may be because of your own attitude which is responsible for it. We often ignore or have dozens of excuses to prove ourselves correct in the wake of any behavior-related problems with others.
- If the situation reaches an irritating level, share your feelings with someone outside your professional area, and if possible, before sleeping, punch your pillow for 15 minutes; this exercise not only gives you sound sleep but you will find enough confidence to face the particular person.
- If you can develop a habit of chewing a chewing-gum every day, you will find that it will become much easier for you to bear the stress in the office, and also it will exercise your teeth as well. The reason behind this is that while chewing it, you will release your anger and pressure without harming anyone or yourself.

Problem No 3 - Acidity Problems Due To Stress

Stress Builder - Every time I eat, I have an Acute Acid attack

Explanation- A series of stressful situations imbalance Acid secretion functions in the stomach, which can lead to medical problems called **GERD** (*Gastro Eshaphogus Reflex Disease*). You must have felt that whenever a stressful situation arrives, you feel like several butterflies are moving down inside your stomach. These problems are also associated with a feeling of passing motions or urinating at urgent. I met a person some time ago who has developed a habit of rushing towards the toilet whenever he found himself in stressful situations.

This is quite common with some of us, as the main reason behind this is that as soon as our brain finds any stressful scene, it prepares the body for a fight or flight response by activating the Neurotransmitters inside our body. These Neurotransmitters activate our body organs to prepare for the coming events, and since the largest number of Neurotransmitters lie in the stomach region, most of us who have poor indigestion problems face this type of problems more severely than other people around. There is hardly any particular medicine available to cure this problem apart from regulating the diet pattern, which includes-

Supportive plans to combat this stress-

- Avoid large meals and try to eat smaller meals throughout the day.
- Avoid Spicy and acidic types of food, which will increase these problems.
- Jaggery has been used in India for a long time for cure of Acid-related problems. If it is used after a midday meal in a small quantity, it can regulate this problem.
- Whenever possible, try to eat in a relaxed manner and in stress-free surroundings.
- Do not stay on an empty stomach for a long time; this will increase the acid formatting in the stomach.
- Take a Cardamom and Clove and crush them together, consume it after each meal. This will, along with an acidity cure, work as a mouth freshener.
- Take around 1 liter of water and add Caraway Seeds(Jeera) to it. Bring it to a boil until half, and drink it warm 2-3 times a day for a week and see the results.
- Mix Black Salt and Ajwyan together, take it after meals and see amazing results.

These measures and remedies are to cure the problems ,but to make it permanent is not a solution in long run.

Remember that -

*If you have an upset stomach, it is not because of what you are
Eating something wrong,
It is because there is something wrong is eating you.*

Problem No 4 - Low Sex Drive and Poor Performance

Stress builder- I am not capable of having good sexual life

Explanations- *S*ex is a vital part of life. It is the basic things in human life like air, water and food. In the Hindu religion, Sex has been given the divine status and is considered an equal form of spirituality, which has been described in all the ancient temples of India. If one has to be forbidden to have sexual pleasure, he would become a danger to himself as well as society. In modern times, we have all the modern facilities to fulfil our sexual needs, T.V., Internet and lots of knowledge and liberty to have our needs, but in modern times, Stress has also created problems in this sector. Researches have shown that people around the world are having problems with their sexual lives. This can be divided into two segments-

1. Low sexual drives.
2. Problems in maintaining errections.

Low sexual drives -

It is really ironical that Sex himself is an excellent stress-buster exercise, that is also associated with multiple health benefits. But in practice, sex is the first thing that is abolished from our lives because of stressful events.

In order to maintain a good sexual life, one must indulge in sexual activities at least 3 times a week. A good Sex not only gives immense pleasure but also has several health benefits, which are not familiar to us because of the social taboo.

Some of the benefits are-

- Sex is an excellent exercise; using all the muscle groups, one can burn up to 300 calories an hour - equal to running 15 minutes on a thread mill or playing a game of squash.

- Endorphin released during sexual process stimulate special immune system cells called - **natural killer cells**, which fight and kill disease cells in the body.

- Blood circulation perks up, which encourages the release of waste and harmful products in the body that can make anyone feel sluggish and ill.

- Sex also boosts the production of testosterone, which leads to stronger muscles and bones.

- Having regular sex can reduce the risk of heart attack as well as improve the blood circulation to the heart, which leads to better heart function.

- Serotonin release during sex, which promotes the afterglow of sex, is the ultimate stress-killer hormone.
- People who enjoy regular sex report a calmer and less stressful life as compared to others.
- Sex causes increased production of Oxytoxin, which is released from the brain, surges to five times the normal level, works as normal painkillers and creates good mood.
- Having regular sex can give you better bladder control and less chance of prostate-related disease.
- And at last- regular sex can give you the ultimate dream - forever young. According to Dr. David Weeks, Clinical Neurophysiologist at Scotland's Royal Edinburgh hospital, who conducted a study on a group of 3,500 people - ranging from 18-102 years, shows that Sex can actually slow down the ageing process, which leads to healthy and younger looks naturally.

Remember that

You change your life when you change your mind.

Supportive plans to combat this stress-

How to say- **Yes** - to sex when you are mentally tired or feel Stressed.

It is very hard to feel sex when there are lots of worries and imaginary stress dominating our minds, but here are some practical remedies which make you wild in bed-

- Try to have dinner early and watch any soft arousal movie with your loved ones.
- Have some aroma therapy candles or insane sticks of lavender and rose; these aromas are known to have some wonderful effects on the human mind.
- Ask your loved one to have some erotic dresses, especially meant for bedtime.
- A sensual massage can create wonders for a dull sex life. If massage is done with Aromatic Oils, it can create wonders. As I have said before, in the Indian context, sex is given the highest form of life because of one reason - it contains all the basic forms of life- ***sound – smell – touch –vision- taste***. Only sex and Mother Earth have the quality to have these senses.
- No matter how busy you are, try to spend at least a weekend dinner with your family. Research has shown that having food together can make the family bond stronger.
- Never mix the alcohol and sex together; a moderate drink can stimulate your mood, but if taken in high quantity, it can increase the desires but reduce the performance, which ultimately can cause depression.

Problems in maintaining erections-

This problem is quite common when the mind is stressed and still the desire of sex haunts the person. In the middle of performance, the mind strikes the agenda of a meeting, and the disaster happens. It is quite common in today's high stress living as the mind regularly involves in the matters which are not needed to be consider.

Supportive plans to combat this stress-

This problem can be overcome by the regular use of yogic exercise, and the one exercise which I recommend for the particular problems are described below-

1. Take a warm shower bath as you are retiring to bed.
2. Use high-fragrance perfumes which can freshen your mind.
3. If possible, take a little exercise - lie down on the bed, close your eyes, and let all the stressful events possibly come to the mind. Keep your breathing in control and let all the problems find their way out of the mind. After 10 minutes, wake up and clap for 10 times in a high tone and then drink a cool glass of water.
4. Milk is a great secret used in India (All Hindi Movies) and works remarkable in this manner. A warm glass of milk at bedtime (around Half hour before) can do wonders.

You will see that the memories of stressful events will not interrupt you during the performance. Some superfoods can help in increasing sexual desires along with physical help.

1. *Carom seeds* - have been used as virility boosters for thousand of years. The seeds contain **Thymol** which increases the sexual desires. A table spoon taken with honey or milk increase the virility and cure premature ejaculations.
2. *Cardamom* - Powdered Cardamom, boiled with milk and downed with a spoonful of honey, is supposed to be a remedy against impotence and premature ejaculations.
3. *Clove* – is considered as an aphrodisiac in China since the third century. Cloves is also famous in Europe for their feel-good facture. Swedish herbalist Ander Mansson wrote in 1642 that if a man drinks milk spiced with five grams of clove would make him desire his wife.
4. *Garlic -* has been used worldwide by ancient Egyptians, Greeks, Romans, Chinese and Japanese. It is an excellent medicine for increasing the sexual performance.
5. *Ginger -* Ancient Indian literature recommends that a mixture of ginger juice, honey and half-boiled egg be taken at night for a month, as a remedy for impotence.
6. *Pepper -* Ancient Egyptians, Greeks, Romans, and Chinese all use this to increase their sexual lives. Daily use of crushed 6 Black peppers in warm milk at bedtime can along with four crushed almonds; it will work as a nerve tonic.

7. ***Saffron -*** It can make erogenous zones even more sensitive. Saffron is a key ingredient in many erotic dishes around the world.

Most of the sexual problems are stated from the stressful mind. You must have noted that when you are happy, you enjoy the sex much better.

Problem No 5 - Early Andropause or male Menopause

Stress Builder-My Sex Desires Has Been Lost Completely As My Age Increases, Is My Stressful Life The Reason Behind It?

<u>Explanations</u>- With age, the production of testosterone, the principal male sex hormone decreases. Lower levels of testosterone and its consequences cause Andropause as men age. Recent international studies show that after 30, testosterone levels generally decrease by one or two percent per year- although this decline can vary widely. Testosterone is the hormone responsible for producing physical characteristics of male puberty and maintaining the features of adult men. It is important for the growth of Bones and muscles and stimulates the bone marrow to make red blood cells.

Symptoms of male Menopause -

Symptoms can vary from one man to another, which may include lethargy or decreased energy, decreased libido or interest in sex, erectile dysfunction with loss of erection, irritability, muscle weakness and aches, loss of sleep, forgetfulness, hot flashes, night flashes, depression, abdominal obesity and thinning of bones or bone loss.

Available treatments -

For the treatment of male menopause, the doctor may prescribe the use of **Hormone Replacement Therapy (HRT),** by which the replacement of male hormones can give significant benefits to older people with the improvement in general well-being, sex drives and functions, muscle mass and strength. But there are certain conditions in which the **HRT** should not be used. It includes Breast cancer and prostate cancer risk, Men who suffer from liver or heart disease, edema, prostate or diabetes problems.

Preventive care -

- It is a fact that a decline in testosterone levels will happen as the age increases. However, the recent studies suggest that smoking and high cholesterol levels may increase the problems.
- Regular exercise will help in maintaining muscle and bone mass.
- Stress and poor attitude toward life are the additional factors to have these problems early. Research demonstrates that men, by and large, are less likely to see a doctor for any reason. Part of it is because of the male psyche, where a dependent role is not acceptable. Generally speaking, men tend to focus less on health and more on money, power and status, and they generally do not go for

consultations till something really goes wrong, but by that time, the little problem is really emerging as a serious one.

To the clinical basis of Andropause, the doctor will check for the following things in men-

- Loss of hair in the armpits and other areas.
- Shrinkage of testicles
- Decreased Libido or low sex drive
- Erectile Dysfunction or Impotence
- Lethargy or tiredness
- Depression
- Decreased muscle strength
- Low sperm count
- Decrease bone density

Androgens basically create "masculinity", and the loss of androgens, such as testosterone leads to physical changes. In men, subtle changes occur in the post-Andropause years. The once-dashing looks are now exchanged for something much less eye-catching. Hardened muscle disappears, and instead, flabby fat accumulates as one gets older. This distorts the physique from an athletic "android" to one with a beer belly and little muscle. The skin also gets dry, and there is hair loss. Hair loss occurs not only in the scalp but also in the genital area as well as in other private parts. The testes also get smaller slowly. There is a loss of height because of osteoporosis, and the spine gets curved from wedge compression fractures. It is important to realize that testosterone can maintain bone integrity just like estrogen in women.

Supportive plans to combat this stress -

- The primary treatment for Andropause is Testosterone Replacement Therapy (TRT). Similar to HRT for women, testosterone replacement works to return normal hormonal levels to a healthy range. Most men report that once on TRT, the symptoms are less frequent and less severe. It should be noted that Testosterone Replacement Therapy does not help with erectile dysfunction (ED) in many men. For men with ED symptoms, you may also want to speak with your doctor about erectile therapies.

- *Be Open-Minded* – There is no shame in having male menopause; it is a natural part of the ageing process for men. Acceptance is a huge part of overcoming some of the psychological symptoms, such as depression and irritability.

- *Keep Busy* – Luckily, the symptoms will pass, and you will be back to your old self. In the meantime, it is important not to withdraw from life, or you may amplify the depressive elements of male menopause. Stay busy, keeping both your mind and body active. Spend a lot of time with loved ones, and even if you are having difficulty with sexual dysfunction, remain intimate with your wife or partner. The intimacy is critical to feeling loved and accepted and keeps you happy internally.

- *It's Not a Dirty Secret* – Talk to your spouse about your male menopause, openly discussing symptoms and issues. Let your loved one know when you are having a bad day, and celebrate the good days together. Having someone by your side while you experience male menopause symptoms will make it easier to get through.

- *Educate Yourself* – Check out websites, go to the library, or join a support group. Do whatever you need to do in order to educate yourself about male menopause. Remember that knowledge is power, and the more you know, the more you can do to help yourself get through it.

The best thing about Male Menopause is that it will not last forever. However, by avoiding the issue and not dealing head-on with the symptoms, depression could get the better of you, and a year could seem like a lifetime. Seek help, reach out to your friends and family, and educate yourself and overall, it will be easier to get through.

Problem No 6 - Severe Heart Burn Sansation And Uneasyness

Stress Builder - I Have Severe Heart Burn Occasionaly, Although My Health Reports Are Normal, Do I Suffer From Heart Disease?

<u>Explanations-</u> Your heart burn may be a reason of Acid Attack, which is medically called Pyrosis. It is a very painful and burning sensations in the esophogus just below the breastbone, caused by regurgitation of gastric acid. The pain often rises in the chest and may followed by the neck, throat or jawline. It can also be associated with the extremely stressful situation where avoiding food at right time or having too much Junk food in the diet creates this situation. Moreover, as I described earlier, constant stress can trigger Acid formation in the stomach. This process not only disturbs regular life events but also creates imbarrasement in public life.

Supportive plans to combat this stress-

Being a Naturopath, I would recommend a diet that is easily available without any harmful effects on the body. By following the simple remedies, you are not only prevent you from this disease but also improve your lifestyle.

What should you avoid -

- Avoid Acidic, Spicy and High-fat food.
- Alcohol, including Wines
- Citrus fruits including Oranges, Lemon, etc.
- Tomato and Tomato Sauce.
- Junk foods- Pizza, French Fries, etc.
- Avoid late-night eating as it harms your digestive system.
- If possible, take a fast any day of the week and just have a liquid diet; it is also good for the stomach.

Eating habits-

- Eat early in the evening, and if possible, go for a light walk.
- Eat larger meals only at Noon and have a light Dinner.
- Try to have hot water after the meals - this will increase the food digitation process.
- Exercise- Obese persons are more prone to have such types of problems; therefore, try to reduce your weight.
- Avoid bending down as it will increase heart burn.
- If this problem persists, have a very simple exercise, which would provide instant relief.

1. Stand behind your office chair and hold it from behind
2. Now, stand on your toes and drop your heels quickly on the ground.
3. Repeat this exercise 20 times.
4. This exercise will revert back your acid back into your stomach, and you will get an instant relief from Heart Burn.

If you still have the problem, you can try to increase the height of your bed under your pillow side so that your acid in stomach will not goes upside when you lie down.

Problem No 7 - Problem Of Sleeplessness Due To Stressful Life

Stress Builder- I Keep Awake All Night In Spite Of My Best Effort

Explanation- A study of medical and drugs claims that data found a 50% increase in the use of sleeping drugs among all adults, fewer than 45, who appear to be using the drugs for a longer period of time to help them fall asleep. The average length of time sleep aids were used by adults under 45 jumped by more than 40%, rising to 93 days in the year 2006 from 64 days in 1998. This study was conducted by the Healthcare business arms of Thomson Reuters. The main cause of this increasing problem is because of increasing stress levels in our daily lives. Further, the sleep specialist at Kettering Hospital of Sleep Disorder center in Dayton, Ohio, states that young people who should have a very strong and healthy sleep system are turning to medications to help with sleep. These results in the use of prescription sleep aids nearly tripled.

Among young adults between 1998 and 2008, Choronic sleeplessness, however, can cause severe health problems like reduction in memory, concentration and problem-solving capabilities to hypertension, heart disease, obesity, mood disorder and frequent infections. Some studies have even linked sleep disorders with cancer and insulin resistance.

A study has proved that people who get fewer than 6 hours of sleep at night are prone to abnormal blood sugar levels, putting them at a high risk of diabetes.

Supportive plans to combat this stress-

The problem of sleeplessness can be solved by certain changes in diet and lifestyle. Here are some of the few tips that will get you a good night sleep.

Diet-

- Avoid heavy dinner.
- Avoid spicy and acidic food at night, which can cause acidity.
- Have dinner at least 2-3 hours before retiring to bed.
- Avoid tea, coffee and chocolates, as they are caffeine-based.
- Have foods that contain carbohydrates, like fruits – pasta, oatmeal and brown rice; they help in producing Serotonin (Sleep Hormone).

- Have milk with one spoon of Honey in it. It is a perfect combination of Tryptophan and amino acids, which promotes sleep.
- Have dark green lettuce, as it contains a compound that helps induce sleep.
- Have foods which contain melatonin, as it induces sleep, which includes Bananas, Plums, Cherries, Ginger, etc.

Exercise -

Although it is really hard to perform heavy exercise when you are tired of your daily routine; it also affects your satisfactory sleep; if mild exercise can be performed, it can create much help.

- Moderate exercise, like aerobics in the morning or early evenings, helps in good sleep. For example, jogging, swimming, jumping rope, or even walking can be a wonder if done only for 20 minutes a day, 3-4 times a week.
- Mild non-aerobics exercises, like breathing deeply, Yoga (Yog Nidra) and light stretching exercises, are also good.
- If exercise is not possible due to a busy schedule, there is an old-age-related exercise to get good sleep.

1. Have a hot feet bath at bedtime; put your feet in mild hot water and cover your head with a towel soaked in cold water on your head.
2. Do these for 15 to 20 minutes daily.
3. You will not only feel relaxed, your tired feet will get pain free from pain, and you will certainly get a good sleep.
4. Do not forget to put a cold towel on your head, as it will prevent you from high Blood Pressure on your head due to hot feet. If possible, you can put a tea bag in the hot water; you'll not only get cure your feet infections but also from the bad smell from your tiring feet.

Aromatherapy -

- Inhale the fragrance of Roses, Lilies or Jasmines at night.
- Add a few drops of Peppermint or Rosemary in your bath water.
- Have sprinkled some of the drops on your pillow at night.
- Have aroma candles at night in your bedroom.

Other remedies -

- Try to have a bath at night before going to bed.
- If you do not feel sleepy, do not go to bed. Remember, the bed is meant for sleep or for Sex only.

- Check out your bed's mattresses or pillows if they are torn out of regular use or become hard enough to support your body, which gives uncomfortable sleep.
- If worries about something haunt you, do one thing - take a piece of paper and write down what exact problem you are having and what possible solution you have got; it clears your mind in some instances and helps you get a good sleep.

Job Related Stress

Problem No 8 - Stress Caused By The Strength Of The Opponent

Stress Builder: My Opponent Is Powerful, I Am Weaker, I Will Definitely Lose!

Explanations- This is a common problem in the workplace. Your colleague is more experienced in the post, and being new to the office, no matter how intelligent you are, an unknown fear about the strength of his personality haunts you. In fact, competitions are the part of life, so rather than frightening, try to adopt some strategies to deal with these emotional problems-

Supportive plans to combat this stress-

- **_Know your abilities_**- In the phase of stressful situations, we often forget our abilities to conquer the situations. Try to find out the exceptional qualities you may possess and try to implement them to rule your opponent.

- **_Know your opponent_**- You may be overestimating his position upon yourself. Try to find out his weaknesses and his expertise. You may find yourself in a better place.

- **_No one is perfect in the world-_** Accept that you cannot conquer your opponent, so rather than stressing yourself, try to find new areas where you can defeat him.

- **_Try to adjust to him_**- The more you get familiar with him, the more your fear declines because we believe that certain conditions are difficult, but when we face those very situations, it seems much easier to handle it than it presumes; it may be possible that his strength may be a tool of your benefit in future. Remember - if you can't win your powerful enemy, try to adjust with him. If you fight, you will certainly lose a lot.

Problem No 9 - Jobs Loss

Stress Builder - I Have Lost My Jobs And I Do Not Know What To Do?

<u>Explanations-</u> This is the ultimate stress level as compared to other stresses we face every day. In a single day, the earning factor for daily bread and butter comes to a halt without any justified reason. It can happen to anybody at any time. Earlier, there was a job security sort of thing, which is quite rare in the world nowadays because of the insecurity in the services. People go to have own businesses, but practically, it is not possible for everyone to do the same. The problem takes a serious matter when the jobless happens to a person in the middle of his career, around the age of 35 to 45. At that age, the ability to find a new job declines and the responsibility increases because the person at that age is obviously married and has kids too who are solely dependent on all their daily requirements on a single man.

This is also a time when a person who is jobless creates lots of insecurity and develops **<u>Negative Self Image,</u>** which develops the interest in dependency on smoking and drinking. Because of the tough competition in the market, employees generally prefer to hire a person of younger age, better qualifications and much ability to perform various tasks at a much lower salary. Under these circumstances, one has to patch up the jobs with a much lower salary, which creates additional stress.

"When one door closes, another door opens, but we often look so long and so regretfully upon the closed door that we do not see the ones which open for us."

Alexander Graham Bell

Faced by the multiple stress factors- from house and from job loss, I remember a short story which is like this-

There was a man living near the coast. He used to be a fisherman, but he lost his boat in a storm. He was highly depressed and did not know what to do? One day, he met a saint and told him the whole story and then asked him to help him. The saint gave him one suggestion - for 2 days in the coming week, there would be a miracle happening on the nearby beach. A magical stone would be coming to the beach, which could turn any iron into gold, so he must search for it and live happily.

That man became so happy by hearing this that he reached the beach one day in advance with the piece of Iron in his hand.

Throughout the day, the man took each and every piece of stone and touched it with the iron, hoping to turn it into gold. One day passed and he found nothing; second day arrived; now, the man became slightly depressed. He started throwing each stone he checks into the water. As time passed, he became so depressed and tired of checking the stone that he took the stone, merely judged it with his eyes and threw the stone without checking it on the iron piece.

*Ultimately, the second day passed without any result. He came back home tired and desperate. The next day, he went to that saint and accused him of making him a fool. The saint listened to him peacefully and said, "**You cannot say that you have not found that magical stone. You indeed took it from the beach, but you were so tired of your failure that you simply threw it into the water without checking it with the iron piece. The energy you have wasted could have become a fortune by doing your work carefully, but you followed your emotions and just cursed your destiny and God.***

This is the same thing when we become so desperate with our failure that we often overlook the new doors that have opened for us. I am not blaming the desperation of job loss, but rather looking back; if we look for new opportunity, we may get better prospects than the previous one.

Coping with the job loss-

- *Turn the loss into an opportunity* – Decide on the way forward and your best attention for the job search. You can go on any dream vacation or meet any far-lived relative.

- *Stay positive and keep an optimistic approach*- Remember that job loss can happen to anyone at any time. You are not alone or an exceptional one in this world. Keep doing exercise, as it will keep depression away and breathing exercises to keep your positive thoughts alive.

- *Do not burn your bridges*- People often make mistakes by forgetting their ex-co-workers under the spell of shame or guilt. But this is a great mistake one can make. Your ex-workers can be your stress reducers by helping you in many ways or by suggesting you any suitable jobs.

- *Maintain your performance*- You have got some free time to improve your abilities and learn something new. This will not only save you from anger and frustrations but by learning new things you have better chances to get a suitable job.

A recent health study determined that there are 3 primary reasons people can't cope in life:
They have a low self-esteem
They live in the past
They don't laugh enough

In fact, the same study concluded that we need a minimum of 12 laughs a day just to stay healthy!

- <u>*Make cash flow in*</u> - If it is not possible to get a full-time suitable job, you can better locate any part-time job. It will not only make you busy but keep your pocket with not sufficient but enough money to live peacefully.
- <u>*No work is Small*</u> - It is really hard, but if you leave your ego on one side and try to start a business from a very small scale, it will be the best choice as one day you will be proud of your decision.

Remember, it is an old saying -

Courage is not always to stand up and fight; it can also be in the form of sitting down and listening.

Problem No 10 - Too Much Work-Related Stress

Stress Builder - I Am Tired Of Doing This Never-Ending Office Work

Explanations- Office is the place where you earn your daily essentials for your family. The office owners are paying you to perform several works to make them earn their bread and butter. So, there is noquestion of saying **No** to the office work. If you start neglecting your office work, it will cause harm to your value to the owner, and eventually, you will lose your job and also the essentials for your family. Earlier, there used to be a regular office hours with no interference at home, but thanks to modern communications, there are hardly any chances to escape - **Mobiles- laptops- and Internet** are the things which can prevent us from reporting to our seniors, no matter where we are.

Now, the question arises: what do we do to prevent us from getting stressed? Here are some remedies to prevent you from getting depressed and stressed.

Stress and worry on the job can be harmful! They cause physical and emotional problems that may damage both your health and your performance. Furthermore, stress grows! Excessive worry is a major element in the vicious cycle of tension: the physical sensations of stress- tense muscles, headaches, insomnia, and so forth lead to catastrophic stress-building thoughts, which in turn aggravate unpleasant physical feelings, and so on up the tension cycle. Soon, just the thought of preparing an assignment or meeting a deadline triggers all the symptoms of stress, along with an overwhelming wish to avoid tasks.

Basic things to remember as a worker in any office -

- Work is worship; the class of a person is evaluated from the quality of his work. If I don't do it, someone else will do the job and take the credit. If I stay focused and take one step at a time, I will make steady progress.

- Divide the entire work in chronological order of steps, attach deadlines to every step, keep realistic boundaries for alterations of deadlines (only if the situation allows), and if possible, delegate work wherever possible. This will not only give you some free time to think about the work peacefully but also some time to relax. Remember, doing all the work by yourself is the quality of type A personality.

- Achievement of targets will make me a hero; if others can, why can't I? If the targets were over-ambitious, others would also not be able to achieve them. Under all circumstances to achieve a target will be highly useful to me. I am going to lift my performance and make it better than my past performance.

- My boss has given me that particular job because he thinks that I am the best person to handle this particular job. I will use all my ability, skills and knowledge to produce results; experience will not come only by observing seniors performing the job; it will come by taking charge of the job, and when my Boss is with me, whatever the problem comes, I will consult my seniors and colleagues.
- *<u>Handle anger</u>*- Often, when the deadlines are to be achieved, even the minor roadblocks start looking like big problems. In such situations, step back and remember that people stalling your work are merely trying to get their own work done. Don't give them more importance than is due to them. Keep deep breathing exercises and try to focus on the problem, rather than focusing on the people who create the problem for you. Think about the solution where you can work without them. Keep in mind that -

Those who can't laugh at themselves leave the job to others.

I don't know where my career is heading: I am absolutely confused and do not know what to do. This is a common situation where there are no promotions or recognition of your work. You should give time to yourself. Ask yourself – what is my goal? Will I be able to achieve my goals following the current path, or do I need to change my act? If you still fail to solve the puzzle, career counseling is the next best option. There is one thing I would suggest-

If the job is not up to the interest but rewards with a high salary, it is worthy.

If the job is not a high salary but you love your job because it is of your interest, it is worth it because it will give you enough satisfaction in life.

But if the job is not paying well and also not up to any interest without the scope of any progress, you are just wasting your abilities and time.

- In the sales profession, employees often say that it is a very tough job as the clients are very demanding. It gives terrible stress in pursuing them for promoting sales. In that case, remember that your client is where your money comes from. In the present competitive scenario, if you want to retain them, then just satisfactory work is not enough; you have to delight them with your work. Also remember that every customer teaches something new to a professional.
- When you feel that things are starting to spin up and get out of control, spend a minute tidying your surroundings – clean your drawers, organize your file cabinet, or declutter your handbag. This simple act works like taking charge of everything you have got; in fact, it is a small task but helps you feel more on top of the world.
- If you are not getting promotions, a feeling of despair naturally comes to mind, but remember that things might have been delayed, but if my performance is reliable, others will be forced to promote me, so under any circumstances, I will not get frustrated.

Because even if I don't get promoted in this company, my good track record will help me get a better position in some other organization.

- **_Guided imagination_** - This is a very good practical exercise to give you relaxation instantly- Shut your eyes and think of any beautiful place- a beach – garden, snow, or any place which delights you. Focus on what you see, feel, smell and touch as if you were there. By using all your senses, you will use your subconscious mind to believe that you are actually there, and you will get ultimate relaxation.

- Research has shown that drinking a cup of tea reduces the stress hormone Cortisol by half if not using more than 3 cups per day.

- **_Stretch yourself_** - When we are under pressure, stress hormones make us slow and sluggish; to prevent this, do physical moments to stop this problem. Dr. Sarah Brewer, the author of Ultimate Stress Buster, suggests that a simple exercise can stop this which is - "stand up and stretch yourself to the fullest possible extent. Shake your hands and arms briskly, then shrug your shoulders. If possible, shout as loud as you can, otherwise, scream silently by opening your mouth widely and forcing your air out."

Nutritional-related advice to keep Stress away-

Includes stress caused by improper diet:

- Caffeine raises the level of stress hormones, making it more difficult to sleep, which makes you more irritable. So do not take excess tea or coffee.

- Bursts of sugar from sweets or chocolates can make you feel more energetic in the short term. However, your body reacts to stabilize abnormally high sugar levels by releasing too much insulin, which causes a serious energy dip shortly after the sugar is high.

- Too much salt raises your blood pressure and puts the body under chemical stress.

- High intake of fats increases cholesterol and body weight, leading to lethargy.

Problem No 11 - Feeling Low Inspite Of Good Life

Stress Builder - I Am Feeling Very Low Nowadays, which Upsets My Life And Gives Me Lots Of Stress. What Should I Do?

<u>Explanation</u>- Regular stressful work atmosphere creates a type of Low esteem syndrome inside our mind. Where change is not possible, or in other words, a favorable atmosphere is not easy to find, our minds tend to accept the problem factors, and the attitude of giving up the fighting spirit dominates the mind. All the things are supposed to do with the physical body, and we tend to ignore the other vital part of our being-emotional health. When feeling blue or emotionally low in esteem, have you ever considered that you might be emotionally unhealthy?

Symptoms of Emotional Imbalance -
- Inability to cope with daily life events.
- Negative thoughts, leading to negative emotions.
- Decline the level of Punctuality. Becomes lazy in daily life.
- Physical illness.
- Disturbed sleep pattern.

And remember one thing in life that -

> *You cannot climb uphill by thinking downhill thoughts.*

Supportive plans to combat this stress -
- Switch to a healthy, balanced diet.
- Make a problem list. Think of ways to deal with problems. Also, evaluate the pros and cons of each option, decide what will be the best option for you and make a plan to deal with it.
- Avoid excess caffeine, tobacco and alcohol.
- Engage in physical activity - if not possible, one quick remedy I generally recommend to my patients is -
    1. Go to any park and try to run as fast as you can, only for a few minutes, increasing it every day. Try to do this exercise for at least one week. After

doing this exercise, you will feel instant relief for achieving something, not physically but on a mental level, and a satisfaction feeling hat you desperately need.

2. This simple exercise would certainly increase the happy hormones level deep inside your mind, which would certainly enhance your bad mood and the attitude of feeling low.

3. We all take 5 types of emotional baggage, which make our life more difficult to travel.

These are -

- **Your Past-** What is done is done; you cannot go back; trying to learn from your mistakes and let them go is the best way to lighten your emotional load.
- **Negativity-** It feels like safety; focousing on negative aspects of life is like holding a bag of rocks on your back, so be positive, and trust yourself and stop having negitive feelings about yourself.
- **Guilt-** Even if you have done your best, things go wrong sometimes. You might feel guilty for that; it happens anywhere, especially when maintaining relationships, so don't blame yourself for that and let it go.
- **Expectations-** It often leads to lots of stress and strife, and mostly, you don't know how much it weigh you down, so forget it, even if you expect it from yourself or from your close relations, be realistic and let it go.
- **Other's mistake -** You may have bad memories of your past, your parents, siblings, friends, etc.; many of us drag around the weight of what others have done, and just as with our own past, the pasts of others cannot be undone, so do yourself a favour and set this extra weigh down.

All these weights in our lives make it hard to live, so think about it, and get rid of these issues, and find yourself a better person.

Remember that -

The True Fact

A person asked God,

What surprises you most about mankind?

God replies,

They lose their health to make more money,

Then they lose their money, to restore their health,

By thinking anxiously about the future,

They forget the present,

Such that they they live.

Neither for the present nor for the future,
They live as if they will never die,
And they die as if they NEVER LIVED.

Lots of people have learned how to achieve in life.
Only a few have learned how to enjoy life.

Problem No 12 - Anger Managemt

Stress Builder- I Cannot Control My Anger Behavior For The People Around Me.

Explanation- Anger is a part of human being characteristic. We have this type of quality in ourselves, which is, on some extent, is a necessary part of our existence. By showing our Anger, we show our rejection and disagreement over any issue, but this thing becomes a regular routine and affects our relationship towards our near and dear ones; it becomes a serious matter. There are two types of angry people in this world: Explosive and Implosive. As Jack Nicklonson tells Adam Sandler in the film Anger Management, "Explosive is the type of individual you see screaming at the cashier for not taking his coupon. Implosive is the cashier who remains quiet day after day, and then finally, shoots everyone in the store." Anger stimulates the release of hormones adrenalin and Cortisol into the bloodstream, which mobilize the body in the short term but can be of highly destructive if applied in a chronic and regular life routine.

There are various triggers for anger ranging from mild irritation to violent outbursts. We tend to behave like machines when it comes to our reactions. Someone says something insulting, and our anger flares up within us, without any moment's gap, just like when you turn on the fan or a light bulb. This whole episode takes around seconds to conceive and ends in regret.

Aristotle said on Anger:

Anyone can become Angry, that is easy,
But to be angry with the right person,
At the right degree, at the right time,
For the right purpose and in the right way is not easy.

There is also a very interesting Quote from **Benjamin Franklin** on anger which says-

Whatever is begun in anger ends in Shame.

It's hard to say but anger is a dangerous thing for the person himself and the person he is dealing with. People with short temper are also prone to heart disease more than the others. There is another theory which shows that a certain group of people belongs to a certain category of personality, which is called the Type-A group. Under this, there are certain characteristics of the personality which are highly stressed-prone and idealistics as compared to others. Also, these specific groups of people are more prone to Deadly Heart Disease and likely to have Heart attack chances by 40% as compared to normal people.

Some of the basic characters of the type A personality are-

Type -A Behavior Pattern	Type- B Behavior Pattern
Talks rapidly.	Handles details patiently, relaxed manner.
Is devoted to work.	Is less competitive with others
Is highly competitive.	Knows his ability factor.
Struggles to perform several tasks.	Has a low concern about time limitations.
Has a strong sense of time urgency.	Doesn't feel guilty about relaxing and have regular planning for Vacations.
Is impatient with idleness	Has a relaxed approach to life
Loses temper easily and violently.	Works at a steady pace and hardly loses his tamper over small matters.
Interrupts others and tries to dominate-taking others while commentating	Take everyone's views before Any important decision.
Always tries to achieve perfection in Every task he performs.	Generally, satisfied with his performance.

There is a very suitable quote regarding this, which says-

He who anger's you conquers you

Now, the question arises how to conquer the anger that controls life and always puts us in a situation that is not acceptable in any form of life. Anger could be triggered by stress, lack of sleep, crash diet and poor water intake. Here are some simple tips to control anger-

How to reduce anger-
- Practice relaxation and breathing exercises to calm down your mind. Breathing is the first thing to be affected by the slightest provocation. By controlling your breathing speed, one can easily control the anger.
- Try to solve arguments by effective communication rather than making decisions in a hurried manner.

- Use problems-solving methods by the use of goal setting and time management; this will reduce the needless pressure on you. For example, we all get monthly bills for telephone, electricity and credit cards, but how many of us pay these bills before the last date? As the last date of paying these bills arrives, the pressure of paying the stress level and anger is at the highest point to absorb.
- Eating well and at regular intervals will keep your energy level in check. Anger due to hunger is most common among those people who perform blue-collar jobs.
- Try to get at least 6-8 hours sleep. Low sleep or inadequate sleep can cause irritation and restlessness.
- Take a break whenever you feel tired. This will not only lift your mood, but also will give you fresh energy to start again.
- Try to maintain a hobby; in your spare time, you will feel refreshed by practicing it.
- Try to avoid smoking in the event of anger; your mind will makes you a chain–smoker, and even you cannot control this habit easily as you become badly addicted to it.
- Communicate with your support system, like family members and your friend circle.
- In the daily life event, try to delegates your work to your friends, family members, and children. It is a bad idea to perform the entire task, whether necessary or unnecessary. This will not only bring additional stress to your life but also Add problems in your relations. Remember, delegating simple work to others would make others feel a sense of responsibility towards you.
- Regular exercise will make you feel fresh and energetic.
- Seek counselling help for conflict in your relations.

Take your life easily, as one has said-

Never take your life too seriously; you will never get alive out of it.

So, accept everything as it comes in life and do not push yourself too hard to deal with it.

Strategies to control Aggression
- Accept that being angry is quite normal, but it should not be harmful to others.
- Try to identify the exact source which makes you angry.
- Shift your focus on what has been done to me to what I can do to prevent myself.
- Never indulge in **Negative Self-Talk;** try to remember your positive qualities.
- Think of more practical approaches to the problems rather than following the same old rational methods to deal with.

- Try to write down your angry thoughts for someone whom you do not like. By writing down on paper, you will empty your poison on the paper and feel much more relaxed.

The only true disability in life is a bad attitude.

I remember a very good story about Aggressive anger, which highlights the results of the quick decision made under the influence of Anger and Stress-

The Red Button

There was a man named Jack lived in a big city with his family. He was working in a big construction company as Chief Engineer, and all the work in the company was under his command. It seemed everything was going well under his control, with good salary, and a loving family, but Jack was not satisfied with the job prospect. His work made him answerable to his boss, whose behavior of dominating nature was a problem for him.

During his office hours, Jack found that by his uncontrollable anger, his boss had begun to dislike him, and he left no chance to humiliate him in front of his colleagues. As it happened one fine day, Jack had some arguments with his boss and returned home earlier.

While retiring home, he was wondering if he could arrange $50,000, he could start a new company where he would be working, and by his experiences, he would certainly succeed. But the main problem was getting that sort of money, which was quite impossible for him to arrange.

As he was entering his house, he met a very old fellow in strange clothes in front of his house. He thought that he might be some beggar or some insane fellow and avoided him under the spell of his bad temper.

At night, around 3 A.M., when Jack got up to drink some water, he was surprised to see the same man standing at the gate of his house, waving his hand and calling him outside. Terrified, Jack decided to meet that old man; he took a stick in his hand and went outside to see him. To the greatest shock of his life, Jack came to know that that old man knew everything about him, his name, his family, and even his desire to own a big company.

He also offered him a help to fulfill his dream by giving him $1,000,00 in cash. Jack was excited and shocked, but the old man offered his help in free of cost by doing him one support, by pressing any phone no. from his diary and pressing the red button of his phone. By doing this, that particular man would die instantly, and Jack would get the money in cash.

Jack thought for a while and his conscious did not allow him to go for it.

In the office, Jack again had heated arguments with his boss, and while retiring to his home, he was full of Anger and Frustration. On the doorstep, he met that old man waiting for his response. Jack, in the wake of his anger, accepted his offer and chose a number from the old man's diary. He instantly dialled the number and pressed the red button. The next moment, the old man handed over the bag full of money.

For a moment, Jack is full of excitement and relief. He thought that millions of people die every day in this world and who would be affected by it. While retiring, the Old man asked for Jack's Mobile Number and began to write down in the same diary from which Jack selected the Number and killed a man recently.

Jack was shocked to see this. He begged the man not to write his name in that diary, but the Old man refused and said - **you have chosen your path and got all you have wanted; I am a helpful spirit who helps people by fulfilling their wishes, but they have to pay for it. You have recently killed a man who was the only earning member of his family for your greed.**

I am going to meet another person in another country who has the same wishes as

You have got. I believe that he will certainly press the red button in Anger and Desperations. He will be doing the same as you have done, and who knows who is going to die? Maybe you, maybe someone else?

By saying this, the Old man disappeared into thin air, and Jack was left alone, deeply shocked, with the bag full of money in his hand.

This Story gives a perfect example of what happens to us when we make quick decisions under the spell of Anger and Frustration, overlooking the consequences of the facts. Jack has got all he wants, but in spite of this his life has become a hell as he has to live under the constant threat of the Red Button untl he dies an early death.

Some Practical exercises to control anger-

- Try to have a chew gum at the time of anger. This will control your anxiety level. Researches shows that gum can reduce anxiety and anger levels by 17% and mild stress by 10%.
- Try to have a glass of cold water at the time of Anger. Water will not only give you cooling effects but also distract you from taking immediate action controlled by your anger.
- If water is not possible to have, try to count from 1to 10 in reverse mode; this will act the same as water.

Some practical tips to stay cool in the crisis-

<u>**The problem factor**</u>- Delay of Metro train on the way to office.

<u>**The remedy**</u>- Lack of control over the situation causes panic and anger. Breathe deeply 5 to 10 times and try to regain control by asking the railway staff about the reason for the delay and the supportive measures available. Forward this whole information and the expected time to reach office to your seniors.

<u>**The problem factor**</u>- The important meeting has started, and you are not prepared well.

<u>**The remedy**</u>- You are worried that you will be shown up and are the first to give the reports and to make an early impression. Sit up straight so that you look and feel well-

prepared for any consequences. Poor body posture will certainly put you highlighted and make you tired and unprepared.

***The problem factor*-** Rushing to hit the deadline in office.

***The remedy*-** You will need more blood going to your head than your stomach, so eat a light lunch and avoid heavy carbohydrates, such as rice, potatoes and other starch-containing food. This will harm your ability to take quick action. Instead, take fruits, like apple, grapes, guava, etc. Think clearly and count all your assets and problems.

***The problem factor*-** Need to leave but not permitted to go because of pending work.

***The remedy*-** Never plan more than 80% of your day in advance. Always make some space for any emergency work or any unexpected assignment. If you decline to stay, you will make bad impressions and harm yourself in the long run in your professional career.

Problem No 13 - Stress Caused By Fear Of Failing

Stress Builder - I Will Fail To Achieve Result

<u>Explanation-</u> Well, the first thing you should understand is that nobody is perfect in the entire world. There is hardly any person in the world who has not failed in his life. There is an old saying-

God makes no mistakes, and that is why he ought to be God.

Failure has an indirect relationship with preparation, which means the more prepared you are, the lesser the chances of failure and its effects. Therefore, have a goal in mind and spend time on preparation to achieve that goal. The more you worry about your failure, the more you will stress. I remember an incident in history when the battle of Agincourt in France was won by a few English worriors against the mighty army of the French Kingdom. You can also read a lot of incidents in history in which mankind has fought and won wars against mighty and powerful enemies. Moreover, if you try to figure out the exact cause of your mistake, you will learn a lot from it, and if you are not prepared, then expecting a good result is unreasonable.

Supportive plans to combat this stress-

In a situation where you are not well prepared, follow the following steps:

- Never keep an unreasonable expectation of succeeding because you know that you have not put in the desired level of effort. Calculate your assets and your weaknesses before taking any important steps.

- Faces the situations; do not go for any escape route which would be harmful to you, with whatever preparation levels you have. If you succeed, praise goes to your smart moves (last-minute groundwork of key matters) and luck, obviously.

- Identify the reasons for your failure, and you will never get stressed. However, sometimes, in spite of being well-organized, you might have a daydream or the negative thought that you will fail. In such scenarios, talk to yourself: "I have given my best in preparations, and unless I am through with the actual situation of the test, I cannot jump to unnecessary conclusions. And one more important thing to remember

- I have read a book called -Your Mind is not your friend, a remarakable book about the mind; it says your mind always seeks the negative side of your life, and you always forget your qualities and worth. The mind is programmed not to see on the other side of the wall. Suppose you accept your fault and see the options left; your mind works in different ways to deal with the problems you are facing and shows many new ways to win.

Never disclose your action plans to your friends/Colleagues, as they may harm your preparations or misguide you in your current action plans.

One last word for the fear of failure-

There are two ways to deal with the problems: you can alter the problems or you can alter yourself to meet the problems.

Problem No 14 - Stress Caused By Having Excessive Helpful Nature. As People Around Misuse It And Put Extra Burden On My Life

Stress Builder - How Can I Say 'NO' To My Friends? What Will They Feel Of Me?

Explanation-: This is the most common problem we all face. Since our childhood, we have been told to help others as much as we can. In every religion in the world, mankind has been directed to help other people as well as all forms of life exist. Being helpful in nature is quite good, but in today's world, where we are surrounded by the much clever people around us, the concept of helping others has become a great tool for gaining stress.

Why do we decline to say NO to anyone, even if it is clear many times that the other person is clearly misusing our qualities, and we are not going to gain anything from it other than problems for ourselves? Basically, I believe that there are two main reasons behind it –

We presume that other people are more superior to us, by physical strength or by financial power. Therefore, we let him dominate us and use us like a carpet on the Floor, and help in his desired objectives at his wishes. We feel that by saying NO, we can lose a good friend who can help us back when needed in the future.

Both are, to some extent, true, but in the context of any incident or relationship, YOU are the most important person available to yourself. Before going to help in such situations, if calculations are made, one can easily understand whether it is wise to go forward or not. I believe that we must have lost several good friends and professional relationships because of helping in other's affairs without our personal interest. Now, the question arises of how to prevent ourselves for not letting others ride us. If we develop the attitude of not helping others, our worthiness in this society will be affected, so we have to maintain a middle path by saving ourselves from being exploited and yet be helpful to others.

Practical Example which I have faced-

A long time ago, when cell calls were costly, I had a friend of mine who has a tendency of not using his mobile phone. Whenever he needed to talk to me, he simply dialled my number and gave me a missed call. For some days, it was bearable, but it started taking my nerves very soon. Although he was a good friend of mine, and I did not want to lose him, still I needed to get rid of this habit.

I started not replying to his missed call and trying to avoid his contact for a few days. He became so desperate to talk to me that he gave me hundreds of miscalls to me, moreover, I picked up his miscalls at the first ring without any answer from my side.

When I confronted him after 2 days, and before I could say anything, he accepted his fault and promised that he would not do this again. Although, this whole incident appearred to be a childish affair, to some extent, my friend knew his fault, and he realized this without harming our relations.

One more example-

I received an invitation to a party some time ago from a friend who stayed near my house. The venue he chose was around 50 km away from my house. It was clearly understood that he had booked that very venue just to save his money. I decided it would be highly foolish to drive all the way just to have dinner in the month of December along with my wife. To me, it is a matter of high stress driving at night as well as security for me and my wife.

I avoided the function and later when came to know from others who had attended the function, that it was a very Stressful experience of their lives. People had faced all sort of problems, like Bad roads, Traffic jams, Extreme colds and fear of life.

My idea of telling you these examples is to consider youself and your family in the first place. Never make any decision that can harm you; no matter what other people think.

Supportive plans to combat this stress-

It is not so easy to say No in every matter because our body language shows the signs of surrender; even if we do not know about this, it is clearly visible to another person. I am describing some techniques to conquer these situations-

If faced the person who is familiar with your helpful habit, try to make a body language cross your arms close to your body tightly, it gives you inner strength to deal with and to defend yourself. This will also give an impression to the person about your declining nature and will not bother to ask for a favor. Try to adopt this body posture as soon as you see him; once you start adopting this attitude, you will find the difference in your life because this posture will also give you inner confidence to deal with tough people.

We tend to fall into the trap of others because we immediately make decisions without thinking twice about the fact.

- Why is my help needed?
- Why didn't he ask anyone else?
- Why should I help him?
- If I help him, what kind of effects does it give on my life?

- If I say NO, what kind of loss am I going to have?

Remember that-

People change when you change your attitude toward them.

These are some of the questions that should be answered before making any commitment. And it is also advisable to take necessary time and discuss this with your family before saying YES,

Keep in mind that-

Being helpful is not bad, but putting yourself in trouble for others sake is foolishness.

Problem No 15 - Unforgiveness

Stress Builders- I Can Not Forgive My Enemies, It Gives Me Great Trouble

<u>Explanations:</u> Unforgiveness is a great stress in today's fast-paced life, where there is a constant race to achieve and survive. Tough competitions often create a scenario where a person intentionally or unintentionally let others down by fair or unfair means. There is hardly anyone among us who has not been backstabbed by a person we know very well.

It is really hard to believe and to accept the backstabbing by a person you know very well. This episode not only gives lots of stress but also affects the pace of work, as most of the time, we have to start from where we began. It is also a very disturbing episode for life as it changes our attitude towards others, and most of the time, we begin to suspect everyone; it affects our relationships at home as well as in the professional sector.

Now. the question arises what to do when there is a great risk of backstabbing, and we are vulnerable to this in spite of our best efforts.

Suggestions-

- Always make an emergency plan for any assignment.
- Never discuss your total plan with anyone in the office.
- Always keep all your project documents in safe custody and check that you have the original keys to your cabinet.
- Never share your computer/ laptop with everyone.
- Keep your computer safe with a strong password and keep it changing frequently.
- Always keep a master copy of any assignment at home.

In case you still get backstabbing, it may be because your enemies are much cleverer than you are or you have taken the opponent lightly. Rather than stressing yourself, you should remember and accept forgiveness because -

Unforgiveness is like a poison drinking himself and wishing that others will die.

It is much prudent advice to you, rather than thinking of taking revenge to analyze your own mistakes in having this problem. It may be because of your own attitude who is responsible for this. Accept your mistake and forget anything that has made you revengeful, as forgiving is the ultimate best policy. And remember that-

True friends stab you in the front.

"Failure is the opportunity to begin again more intelligently."
Henry Ford

Stress Caused By Personal And Family Problems

Problem No 16 - Financial Problems

Stress Builder- I Don't Have Any Good Source Of Income; I Have To Pay Huge Credit Cards Bills And Other Payments. I Don't Know What To Do?

<u>**Explanations**</u>: In such situations, think how much effort you have really made to generate any income. Are you looking for another good job or waiting for a miracle to happen? It may be possible that you are looking for some debt payments form a friend that are expected to be in your hands very soon. There are several other possibilities which have made you accept a loan from credit cards or spend lavishly without thinking wisely. Before you feel stressed, have you made a list of -

- How many companies have I actually applied to?
- Why am I being rejected in interviews in spite of my best efforts?
- Where can I arrange for the pending bills of my spending?

Find out the weaknesses within you and work over them instead of thinking negatively. In case you are waiting for some bigger opportunity, have faith in your decision-making. But if you feel that you have waited for too long, start working to support yourself with your eyes set on the bigger opportunity. In practice, depending on other sources other than your pockets is foolish. I remember a very old story which resembles the problems of financial stress made by our poor attitude. Remember, the strength of a man is judged by his flexibility.

3 brothers

In the remote area, there was a village where 3 brothers lived happily with their families. They were leading a very happy life, but one year, the drought struck the village. People began to die because of starvation. 3 brothers did their best to survive, but ultimately, their resources faded.

They became so desperate by starvation and poor conditions that they thought to commit suicide by jumping into the valley. They were climbing in desperation and met a saint sitting on the edge of the valley. The saint asked them about their desperations and offered them help.

The saint told them that he had found some bags full of gold and silver coins on the hill, and it could be used by the 3 brothers, as nobody dared to go up to that height. He also warned them to take only what they needed. If you dare become greedy, you will have to pay for it.

The 3 brothers happily started climbing the mighty mountain. After climbing for several days, they found a bag full of silver coins. The elder brother found it sufficient for his family and descended with it. The remaining 2 brothers continued their journey, and after some time, they found a bag full of gold coins.

The middle brother suggested to the younger brother that they had gotten more than they deserved and should go back to their family, but the younger brother was not satisfied with it. He simply refused and continued his journey in search of a much better fortune.

After climbing for several days, he reached the summit and found that a man was sitting there with a giant wheel spinning on his head. That wheel was making a loud noise and creating a lot of sufferings for that man.

The younger brother was highly surprised, and as soon as he asked that man about that wheel, the giant wheel immediately shifted its position from the man's head to the younger brother's head. He cried with pain and trouble. The man, whom the wheel was spinning on his head, found deeply relaxed and explained to the younger brother- I came here in the same manner as you do. I was also very much greedy and restless nature, as you are. I ignored the request of my brothers and came here to ask the person who was sitting here with the same wheel on his head. I got the wheel on my head by asking the same questions you asked me. Now, all you have to do is to wait here and let someone ask the same questions, only then you will get relief from here.

This little story clearly indicates the true picture of the greed which we have got. We tend to make useless excuses to spend more without looking back at our pockets, and when we strike deeply into the credit, we feel stressed rather than changing our attitude. Unlike the story, we all have a spinning wheel over our heads and wish that others would ask us and take the wheel on our heads. But this is not possible every time.

Supportive plans to combat this stress-

- What is done is done; rather than cursing yourself and your family members, you should make a list of the things which can bring you out of this mess.
- Make a list of the efforts which can prevent you from taking credits or measures to keep your bills into the sustainable amount.
- Try to make a list of the activities by which you can save your limited money, which can be utilized in future.
- Try to utilize your spare time in some part-time work for additional income.

Remember that-

You really have to look inside yourself and find your inner strength, and say,
I am proud of myself and who I am, and I am just going to be myself.
- By Mariah Carey

Why Everyone Is So Stressed Nowadays

Suppose Mr. **A** is stressed in the morning because of his professional problems. He shouts at his wife on very small issues and stresses her in the morning; he again shouts and stresses his driver on the way to his office. At the office, he again follows the same temperament by shouting at his junior staff. He is still stressed, but he has created a lot of people around him who are deeply irritated and stressed by his behavior.

If we notice all these people who have been stressed by Mr. A would eventually release their anger on other people, for instance-

- His wife releases her anger on the house maid –who takes this problem to his family and releases his anger on his husband and children.

- His driver gets irritated and shouts at his fellow drivers on the way.

- His staff releases their anger on the customers or fellow workers or takes it home as a gift for their Family members.

So, at last, there is a series of lot of stressed people, who are creations of a single fellow named Mr. A. If Mr. A would have absorbed his problems and remained cool, there would not be any problem for anyone.

I believe that this is one of the major causes of growing cases of stress-related problems around the world. If we accept the stress and do not stress others, the problems can be tackled very easily.

Problem No 17 - Relationship Problems

Stress Builder: I Just Cannot Adjust With My Spouse; I Think He/She Tries To Dominant Me And Moreover I Feel Neglected

Explanations: We are life partners, but we are two different persons, so obviously, we have different perceptions. Only we can solve our problems; outsiders cannot. We often neglect his personal existence as we tend to ignore it for our own personal needs. All personal matters require sufficient time and attention, and we realize what we expect from each other. We need to decide on certain haves and don'ts, and the misunderstanding will automatically vanish. We all face some sort of marital disputes in our lives, and mostly, we start with the wrong calculations and over-expectations.

Man is a social animal. We all make family to protect us and give us moral support as well as emotional and sexual needs. It is not possible for any man to get rejected from the family front and also face rejection from his professional front. It is ironic that most of the suicides are conducted by the family man rather than the bachelor persons.

When a man finds rejection from his spouse, the stress level rises to the a dangerous level because, along with stress, man tends to develop a habit of dependency on smoking and drinking, which makes the problems worse. The habit of taking unnecessary risks also develops among younger males, which sometimes proves fatal and ends in an early death.

Now, the basic questions appear that from where should one starts? Dealing with your spouse in a rough manner, is highly dangerous as it can open a Pandora's box with never-ending problems to handle. This results in Divorce, which is the highest stress creating in the stress chart. It can not only ruin you financially, but you have to bear social rejection and can lose your image in public. I personally believe that the episode of divorce can

Puts a man 10 years ahead of his age and also puts him 10 years behind in his financial status.

Also, there is no perfect remedy by getting divorce, as there is no guarantee that you will find a suitable or much perfect match as you are having now. I believe that most of the people, rather than going for counselling themselves, opt for divorce as they think that they will find a much better match next time. And when they realize the mistake, it is too late to say sorry. And if the children are also a part of the family, the case becomes more complicated and disastrous. The future growth of the children are highly depends on the existence of father. In the absence of a strong hand upon the growth of children, it is highly affected and proves to be a disaster for society also.

I believe that I have expressed my views enough, and I should come to the remedy sections. I am going to describe some easy and practical remedy to solve these problems-

Try to share some time together, no matter how busy you are. Most of the problems start when the lack to time cuts the communication between two people. Try to spend an evening together on a dinner, or if possible, take a break and go out for a weekend trip and when you come back, find the difference.

Talk about the problem factors together. There may be simply a communication gap, which is the basic cause of all the mental stress between you two. But one important advice - do not talk about the problems in your home, as there may be some atmosphere pressure that prevents you from talking clearly, and the whole concept ends up in a big fight. If suitable, go to any public place or a café because, in a public place, it is not possible to use any hard words which can create a public scene. Keep in mind that compromise is the best thing for a man because

My wife and I always compromise. I admit I'm wrong and she agrees with me.

Your old photo albums/CDs of your marriage/party or any family celebrations are the best source to make up your mood, and by remembering your happy times, you can forget your current problems for a while and make youself stress-free.

Find out the area where your spouse dominates you. It may be because she can handle the situation better than you do; if you feel so, accept this, and because it is the worst part of the man's character to accept his wife as much superior. Remember that every person has their own qualities, and being a lady, it is in her gender to perform certain tasks much better than the male counterpart.

I haven't spoken to my wife in years. I didn't want to interrupt her.
-Rodney Dangerfield

I believe that I have given you enough stress by explaining to you some of the things you
Might dislike (But it is a fact), so here are some of the jokes I have collected, from various sources, which makes your mood lighter and slightly stress-free.

- What is the difference between men and women? A woman wants one man to satisfy her every need. A man wants every woman to satisfy his one need.
- Why don't men often show their true feelings? Because they don't have any.
- What's the difference between a man's wife and his girlfriend? Around 60 Pounds.
- What's the difference between government bonds and men? Bonds mature.
- What's the difference between a man and E.T.? E.T. phoned home.
- Why do men like commercials? You can't believe a word they say.
- Why are men like popcorn? They satisfy you, but only for a little while.
- Why are men like blenders? You need one, but you're not quite sure why.

- What do men and women have in common? They both distrust men.
- Why is a man like old age? They both come too soon.
- A man and woman both jumped off a high building; who'd land first? The woman. The man would get lost on the way.

Now back to the main topic-

In the event of a stressful life between partners, man often tends to find his emotional and physical satisfaction from other sources such as extramarital relations or sexual satisfaction from professional sex workers. This scenario makes the case worse as it is almost impossible for man to hide these acts from his family in the long run.

Having an extramarital affair can cost you more than your marriage. It can be fatal because the strain of juggling married life and the secret lover leads to additional stress and tension for the cheating partner, which can lead to migraine headaches, can cause a potentially fatal aneurysm, or ballooning of the blood vessels in the brain. This study was presented by Neurologist Lorenzo Pinesssi, president of the **Italian Migraine Society**, at the international conference in Turin.

Neurologist Lorenzo Pinesssi and his team studied hundreds of patients across Italy who reported migraines. Some of the patients are the one who indulge in the extramarital affairs are having the worst medical status as compared to the other persons who are not involved in any type of affairs. It clearly shows that having extramarital affairs can put extra burden on the body which in long run can prove fatal.

Also, finding sexual satisfaction from professional workers can be the deadliest as there is a great risk of getting Sexually Transmitted Disease (STD). Which can turn life into hell? Are you ready for It?

Some Practical Remedies To Improve Your Negative Imaginations Towards Your Spouse

After retiring from office tries not to go home directly. Try to spend some time alone in the park and relax yourself. There may be chances that you go home directly from office and take all the office stress in your mind, and you discharge all your anger and frustrations to your family, which makes the relationship problems and your image affected. I read quotations from a Tibetan book that say that there is a tradition in the Tibet for this problem. A person retiring from his work is supposed to take a 5 round of his house running at full pace before entering his house. The main motive of this exercise is to shake all your stress before entering your house.

Married persons are more prone to stress because they feel that they are lonelier now after the marriage before they were married. Because of the emotional imbalance, they easily tend to develop a dependency profile. To these problems, there is a very simple exercise to perform.

If you have any reliable source of friends, try to share your feelings and seek guidance. If not possible, try to seek professional help in counselling to ease the problem. If this is also not possible, do these simple and effective exercises, which can be highly effective in overcoming the problem of loneliness -

- Go to a park and hug a tree suitable in your arms, tell it about all the problems and seek help from it. Do this for a few days, and you will certainly feel a positive change in your behavior and the problem.

This is the most practical exercise, which can give the warmth of a relationship as well as a release of the pressure that builds up in the mind for expressing stress and relaxation, which comes automatically by the release of the pressure. Believe me, this exercise for relaxation and stress removal has been found very much effective by some patients of me, who have the problems of marital disputes.

Problem No 18 – Smoking Cigarette

Stress Builder- Whenever I Feel Stressed I Start Smoking

Explanations- Smoking is the worst side-effect of everyday stress. The slightest provocation of stress or any other problems makes a man strike his cigarette packets and lighter. The mind of a chronic cigarette smoker is developed in such a manner that it can not absorb any type of pressure in his mind.

Tobacco smoking is the major cause of mortality around the world. It is not only a health hazard but also an economic and social hazard.

There are different categories of smokers around the world-

- **Positive effects smoker**- He is the one who enjoys smoking at his ease. He enjoys every puff and receives pleasure in blowing smoke rings.
- **Negative effects Smoker**- He is the one who smokes in times of crises and stress arousal, such as nervousness, anxiety and anger.
- **Addictive smoker**- He is one who smokes to satisfy a carving or to solve a problem.
- **Habitual smoker**- He is a chain smoker. He smokes without any justified reasons and without consciously aware that he is smoking.

Hazards of smoking-

- Cause Cancer and degenerative diseases, such as (COPD) Chronic Obstructive Pulmonary Disease and Coronary Artery Disease (CAD)
- Increase the risk of premature hardening of arteries, resulting in angina and sudden death, along with the risk of Stroke - Paralysis.
- Tendency of hypertension and clot formations, which can be fatal as the age increases.
- On an average, the smoker dies 15 years earlier than a non-smoker.
- Recent studies conducted in universities or Iowa suggest that smoking is also associated with premature ageing.
- Another study conducted at the Chicago University claims that cigarette smoke perks up levels of stress hormones in the heart that can reshape the left ventricular, the heart's main pumping chamber, and increase the levels of the

activated forms of enzymes in the heart muscles which leads to disfiguring the heart.

- A cigarette is a deadly combination of over 4000 different deadly chemicals; some of them are the deadliest for the human body.
- In women, smoking is an easy way to develop breast cancer because Breast epithelial Cells and the cancer cells have nicotine receptors, which can increase cell growth and migration in the presence of Nicotine.

I believe that rather than making a list of the adverse effects of smoking, I should describe the practical and easy way to quit smoking for the benefit of the health.

***Think hard*-** When you pick up a cigarette, just ask yourself why you are smoking. This will certainly make you think twice before lighting the cigarette.

***Stop it now*-** If you are planning to stop smoking, make up your mind and stop it now.

***Create ambience*-** Go for complete health checkups; you will certainly know what and how much damage you have created to your health. Go for dental checkups also to see the tobacco spoils on your teeth. Throw away your ashtrays and avoid standing in the groups where most of the people are smoking. You will be surprised to know that a smoker's mind is so much set on the smoking habits that it will reach the point of smoking the number of cigarettes from where he quit.

***Relaxation techniques*-** Deep breathing, yoga, walking and staying busy will certainly help combat this problem.

***Take substitute*-** In case you feel an urgent urge to smoke, try different options like candy, chocolate, chew gum, etc.

***Power of one*-** Buy one cigarette at a time instead of buying a full packet. If you plan to quit, try to buy another brand of cigarette or throw away your cigarette by taking one or two drags.

***Keep on trying*-** It is not possible that you may succeed in a single time, but there is no need to feel guilty; you can try another time with more determinations.

***Try another brand*-** This is a method for quitting. In fact, you have been using a single brand for ages, but if you really want to quit, just ask for any unfamiliar brand. Whenever you smoke, the strange taste of the new brand will certainly make you feel bad about smoking, and you will hardly finish the whole stick.

One very simple exercise if you do, take a straw (used for drinking cold drinks) and a glass of very cold water; whenever you feel the urge, just drink water from the straw; in your unconscious mind, it gives the same soothing pleasure as of a cigarette.

Quitting is not very difficult; if you are determined to do so, no one on earth can let you smoke again.

Problem No 19 - Excess Drinking

Stress Builder - I Can Not Quit Drinking in Spite of My Best Efforts

<u>Explanations</u> - There are different types of alcohol drinkers in the world. We probably know only two types of drinkers in general, but the British health officials now acclaim that there are nine different kinds of Drinkers in the world. The British research to promote public health campaigns against drinking may help the authorities to prevent excessive drinking in a society that is already facing acute problems due to underage drinkers who drink their way to the hospital each year.

The nine personality types of heavy drinkers are-

- <u>*Destress drinkers*</u>- They use alcohol to regain the control of their lives and to calm down. It generally includes the middle-class men and women, who drink in the case of extreme desperation and depression.

- <u>*Conformist Drinkers*</u>- they are driven by the need to belong and seek a structure to their lives. They are men aged 45-59 in clerical or manual jobs.

- <u>*Boredom Drinkers*</u>- They consume alcohol to pass the time, seeking stimulation to relieve the monotony of life. Alcohol helps them to feel comfortable and secure.

- <u>*Rebounding Drinkers*</u>- They are driven by the need to keep in touch with people who are close to them. These types of drinkers are not habitual, and they tend to drink only when the group makes a plan to assemble.

- <u>*Community Drinkers*</u>- They are motivated by the need to belong. They are usually lower-middle class men who drink in large friendship groups. These types of people usually cross the limit of their tolerance and create several problems for themselves as well as for others.

- <u>*Hedonistic Drinkers*</u>- They have stimulatation and want to abandon control. They are usually divorced people with grown-up children who want to stand out from the crowd.

- <u>*Macho Drinkers*</u>- They spent most of their spare time in the pubs. They are mostly men of all ages who want to show their Macho and High Tolerance approach to the world.

- ***Borders Dependents*** - They regard the pub as a home away from home. They visit it during the early day and almost every evening, drinking fast, and often do not retire to their homes to spend their time anywhere they like. These types of drinkers are the worst types of drinkers as they create lots of stress for themselves as well as for their families.

Problems of drinking-

Chronic alcohol abuses the life by 15 years or more not only due to the heavy damage to the health but also to the poor attitude towards life. It has been reported in the studies that the alcoholics have a higher death rate than non-drinkers. A study published in an Indian health journal in 2007 revealed that 65% of the total hospital population is suffering from metabolic syndrome, like the Pot Belly, Hypertension, diabetes, high bad cholesterol and low bad cholesterol. This is serious as compared to the male patients as they are more prone to the problems of Lack of exercise, faulty diet and consumption of less fruits and drinking excess alcohol in spite of medical warnings.

There are also additional health problems associated with excess alcohol drinking-

- ***Hypertension-*** Increase in the blood pressure or regular fluctuations in the blood pressure.
- ***Palpitations-*** Tachycardia, irregular heart rates, VT-(ventricular Tachycardia), VF- **(Ventricular Fibrillations)** which may leads to sudden deaths.
- ***HNS-Holiday Heart Syndrome-*** This is because of the irregular heart rate at weekends after consuming heavy alcohol.
- ***H F-*** The danger of the Heart failure.
- ***S C D-*** Sudden Cardiac Death.
- ***C M P-*** Excess alcohol may cause damage to the heart muscle. **Cardio-Heart-MP-Mayopathy** means the muscle dysfunction.
- ***Increased TG-*** Excess drinking may lead to the increase of high bad cholesterol or triglycerides, which leads to increased obesity and metabolic syndrome.

It also increases the risk of cancers in the following regions of the body:
- Oral
- Food pipe
- Stomach
- Liver
- Lungs
- Breast, etc.

It increases the uric acids and decreases the Magnesium in the body.

It is the gateway to the smoking - consumption of faulty junk foods, health drain, and wealth drain. It has no benefits to overall health potential.

Alcohol is both a stimulant and a depressant; it increases the level of serotonin for a while and then causes the depression.

It is the main cause of the damage of the liver, the most important part of the stomach.

Remedy for all these problems-

Now, you may be aware that the consumption of alcohol is the ultimate damage one can do to his body. How to prevent yourself from these heavy losses is the main cause. So, here are some of the remedies; by practicing these, you can -

- Try to make yourself busy by spending your time with your family. The family bond will prevent you from taking unnecessary drinking.
- Try to drink in a moderate amount.
- Try to face the problem which leads to drinking. Drinking is not a substitute for any problem.
- Switch on to other drinks as there are several other drinks available in the market which can give enough pleasure without causing much damage to the health.
- Do plan for the event that leads to the drinking or the group which leads to unnecessary drinking: try to avoid these for your health's sake.

The solution to this kind of stress is a complete diet chart for the entire week along with just half an hour of exercise every day. The best exercises are: jogging, skipping, stretching exercises, stomach exercises, push-ups, pull-ups and breathing exercises.

Ladies Oriented Stress Problems

Health Problems Due To Stress

Problem No 20 - Depressions Due To The Extreme Stress

Stress Builder-Whenever I Feel Stressed, I Get Depressed

Explanations: Let us consider a scene where a patient walks into my clinic and says that she has been feeling sad and depressed for the last 3 weeks. The main reason behind this is that her fiancée has left her for another woman. She has not been sleeping well since then, her appetite is poor, and she has lost her interest in all of her usual activities. Now, the ball is in my court. Should I give her a clear diagnosis of clinical Depression? Or is she merely experiencing what the 14th-century Monk **Thomas Kempis** called?

"The proper sorrow of the Soul."

Psychiatry has medicalized normal sadness by failing to consider the social and emotional context in which people develop the low moods. In the recent book: the **Loss of Sadness** (Oxford-2007), Allen Horwitz and Jerome Wakefield asserted that for thousands of years, symptoms of the sadness that were **with cause** were separated from those that were **without cause**. With the help of modern diagnostic criteria, modern consultants often diagnose the patient's complaints and related to the symptoms, like poor appetite, insomnia, low energy, and hopelessness as depressions. Most of us can point out the recent losses as disappointment in our lives, but it is not always clear whether it is causally related to our becoming depressed or it is just a normal sadness.

As in the modern times, Depression has been linked to all our mental problems without knowing the exact cause of it. As far as the easiest and the most understandable definitions of depression are concerned, let us consider an example-

Suppose a person lost his new mobile phone; what should we expect from his behavior-

- **Denial-** He will simply deny the lost and keeps searching for it all over the place.

- **Anger-** When he does not find it anywhere, he simply becomes angry and revengeful.

- **Blame-** When he does not find any suitable person for anger, his mind quickly turns into the blaming format - suppose he lost his mobile in a party; he would blame the host of the party for the loss because of his poor management. To come to this session, the mind changes its statement several times and blames more than several people for his loss.

- **Helplessness**- As time passes, the loss is known to several people around that particular person. When the recovery of the phone is almost impossible, the concept of Helplessness stricks the attitude.

- **Acceptances**- Finally, a person accepts that his mobile has been lost. This whole episode of loss takes about several days to one or two weeks. This is the final stage of the loss section and also the beginning of depression. If the problem of remaining sad continues till after and the daily activities affect up to a dangerous level, then it can be defined as the perfect case of Depression. Depression can occur as a result of the death of loved ones, misfortune, physical ailments and material losses. It is a feeling that turns into a disease over time. Depression has several dimensions, depending on the reasons why it appears in a person's psyche and in the way it is reflected in the person's behavior.

We all consider all our daily activities of stress-related problems to be the depression syndrome, which is not right. As far as my case is concerned, I would certainly go for the sad attitude because of the loss. In most of the cases, the simple remedies of Sadness can cure the patient as He/She has just forgotten about the ways to be happy and a lot of negativity has just overcome his mind.

To me, reducing the negativities from his mind is the ultimate remedy to his sadness. In the events of Sadness and Depression, we all tend to forget the blessings we all have been provided, for example, the first blessing is a healthy body which is, in fact (To most of us) disease-free, and we should be proud of it. If we calculate all other blessings that belong to us, we may find that the current state of mind about the particular problem is useless, and it is not worth being sad.

To overcome regular intervention from the events which lead us to the Sadness/ Depressions, we must conduct regular relaxation exercises to control our minds.

Take a few minutes from our daily schedule to create and affirm the mental ground to clear all the useless worries from it. I am going to explain a good exercise which is highly beneficial in this current problem:

1. Sit in a quiet room and in a relaxed manner. With hands at your side or on the laps. Now close your eyes and start breathing lightly and easily. Let your attention follow your breath. Continue this exercise for two to five minutes, just closing your eyes and focusing your mind on easy, natural breathing.

2. Do let all the useless events come into your mind and focus on them to vanish from the mind forever. If you find it hard finding yourself in concentration, you can use the soft music for better focus, as the music is also known as a stress reliever.

3. Focusing on the breath means keeping the mind alert and free from the clutter; the mind often wanders like an untamed monkey, so this exercise trains the mind to develop focus and concentration.

4. Meditation is concentration. It is not focusing your mind to be quiet; it is finding the quiet that is already there.

5. As you meditate regularly, you will find an appearance of youthful energy and vitality, and calmness in the mind, which is your restless mind so often carves for.

Benefits-

- This type of meditation causes deep relaxation at the nervous system level, at the muscle level and in the internal organs. Our heart fraction improves and even our cholesterol level improves. It has been observed that since tension in the arteries is reduced, blood pressure is also regulated and overall the general well-being is felt instantly improved.

- Day to day stress is managed efficiently through meditation; 5-10 minutes of meditation is recommended for persons who are sick or burdened with responsibilities or pressure for time.

- Meditation distressed the mind. The mind is able to be concerned better, and there is greater clarity in thoughts; regular practice equips the mind to deal with life's problems calmly.

- The heart rate and the respiration rate slow down; this results in efficient working of the heart and lungs. When the mind is relaxed, there is a better balance in the body as the cells work in harmony and provide benefits to the body.

- Those who are meditating for the first time register a decrease in beta waves (the frequency range of brain activity above 12HZ), a sign that the cortex is not processing information as actively as usual. After the first session, People show a decrease in beta wave activity.

- ***<u>Why to meditate for depression</u>***- A recent study was jointly carried out by the scientists from the University of Exeter and the King's College London. It is published in the Journal of Consulting and Clinical Psychology. The eight-week study included people who had suffered from chronic depression and were divided into groups; half received the antidepressant medicines, and the rest were treated under the Mindfulness Based Cogitative Therapy.

After 15 months of trial, 47 of those given MBCT therapy reported a high quality of life and less depression symptoms as compared to the other group. Many of the exercises were based on the Buddhist Meditations, and while the antidepressant reduces the symptoms of depression, most patients remain vulnerable to a reversion. But MBCT teaches people skills in life.

Meditations And Brain Waves

There are four different types of Brain wave in our mind-

1. **Beta Brain Wave -** The beta brain wave state is your conscious state of mind. At beta, your eyes are open, and you are wide awake and alert. In this state, you are able to live, focus and do your day-to-day activities. Beta helps when you attend a meeting, play sports or do an activity that requires you to concentrate. Notice the difference in performance in these activities if you have overslept, turn up tired or are under stress. In these states, the Beta brain wave levels are not at their peak performance levels.

2. **Alpha Brain Wave** - When you are truly relaxed, your brain activity slows from the rapid patterns of Beta into the more gentle waves of Alpha. Your awareness expands. Fresh and creative energy begins to flow. Fears vanish. You experience a liberating sense of peace and well-being. It is at this level of the Alpha Brain Wave where stress melts away without any effort. The Alpha Brain Wave state is the key state to be in for stress relief. All <u>stress relief techniques</u>, whether they are Western or Eastern in orientation, try to access this Alpha level of mind. Being in the Alpha Brain Wave state helps you tap into your creativity and is excellent for problem solving, finding new ideas and practicing creative visualization. Alpha can be used to attain deep levels of relaxation that are essential to your health and well-being.

Alpha brain waves range between 7 and 12 HZ. This is a place of deep relaxation, but not quite meditation. In Alpha, you begin to access the wealth of creativity that lies just below your conscious awareness - it is the gateway, the entry point that leads into deeper states of consciousness.

3. **Theta Brain Wave** - Going deeper into relaxation, you enter the mysterious Theta state, where brain activity slows almost to the point of sleep, but not quite. Theta is the brain state where magic happens, and many of the mystical experiences with meditation occur. Theta brings forward heightened receptivity, flashes of dreamlike imagery, inspiration, and long-forgotten memories. Theta can bring you deep states of meditation.

A sensation of "floating" and, because it is an expansive state, in the Theta brain wave state, you may feel your mind expand beyond the boundaries of your body. Theta is the ideal state for super-learning, re-programming your mind, dream recall, and self-hypnosis.

Theta brain waves range between 4 and 7 HZ. Theta is one of the more elusive and extraordinary realms we can explore. It is also known as the twilight state, which we normally only experience fleetingly, as we rise up out of the depths of delta upon waking, or drifting off to sleep.

4. **Delta brain wave** - The Delta brain wave pattern is seen in your deep sleep. It is the level where you recharge your batteries and wake in the morning feeling wide awake and refreshed. Delta brain waves are most frequently produced by your brain while you are in deep sleep. They are the deepest frequencies that your brain produces, and they have been related to states of DEEP RELAXATION, extremely calm and soothing mind states.

Delta has also been linked with an increase in the body's production of growth hormones, which plays a vital part in the body's natural ability to heal and rejuvenate. Delta is the ideal state of healing and rejuvenation. It is very hard to meditate in this state, as you will often fall asleep. This is the area of the Eastern Mystics, Yogi's and Monks. It may take years of meditation to achieve this level.

- Also, your adrenal glands produce less Cortisol, your mind ages at a slower rate, and your immune function improves. Your mind also clears, and your creativity increases. People who meditate regularly find it easier to give up life-damaging habits, like smoking, drinking and drugs.

Some facts about the Meditations

Ancient facts-

- Nobody knows when the meditations started. Experts say it may have begun thousands of years ago, like all other mystical practices. It might have been reserved for tribal shamans, who were believed to be in touch with the spirits.

- 2000-3000BC- Vedic Traditions- Meditations are described in ancient Hindu texts; they have been part of the religion and its many offshoots ever since.

- 588-BC- Buddha- After meditating under the banyan tree, Prince Siddhartha achieved enlignment, and Buddhism was the result.

- 2nd Century AD - Christian Meditations- A group of Christian Monks known as Desert Fathers retreated from the world to live in simplicity. They meditate to get closer to God, and more than 1000 years afterwards, meditation would be an increasingly important part of the Christian practice.

- 1000 AD- Muslim Meditations- the Muslim section known as the Sufis (after the plain wool garments, called 'SUF", which they wore) also incorporated meditations into their rituals of worshipping.

Other benefits of Meditations-

Studies done by the universities in US, Europe and India show immense benefits of meditation on many levels of life, some of them are-

- Greater order line of brain functioning.
- Improves the ability to focus and creativity.
- Increase the level of relaxation and decrease the level of stress hormone.
- Increase the level of intelligence.
- Natural change in breathing.
- Lower high blood pressure.
- Reversal of the ageing process.
- Reduce the need for medical care.
- Controlled /decreased addictions.

The needs for meditation for the stress-related depressions; it makes the mind to relax and the view to see the world. This is the most inexpensive and effective remedy for the disease, as there is no medicine in the world to change the attitude we see the world.

Problem No 21 - Menstrual Problems

Stress Builder-I Have Very Irregular Periods. Is It Due To High Stress?

<u>Explanations-</u> Problems of Monthly cycles can be divided into two segments-

<u>Irregular Monthly cycles</u>- This is one of the most common problems faced by the women of today. It can be a major stress-related disorder of modern times, which affects the most of the women in any instance.

The Hormonal System

A normal functioning system is totally pain-free and without any discomfort, including the hormonal system of the body. When stress changes your brain chemistry, the hormonal system is the next in line to become affected. The cycle then swings greater than it should, which creates all the hormonal irregularities.

This can be even more damaging if you are pregnant. Regular Stress can affect the secretion of the hormones of the body, which not only regulate the normal functions of the body but also play an important part in the development of the pregnancy and the menopause facture in the later years. Since in the today's world, women equally play the roles of working and the homemaker, they are more prone to face stress as compared to the man counterpart.

Researche has shown that involving the international comparison of women in 37 different populations and cultures, career women are more likely to have androgynous figures, which indicate a higher level of androgens, as opposed to estrogen, which is vital for conceiving successfully. The modern women are more prone to these types of problems because of their successful careers and a high level of stress, which can also damage their chances of having children. The females who are driven to succeed suffer a hormonal shift with also a change in the pattern of monthly cycles.

In the recent times, it has been found that the problems of menopause are shifting to the years of as early as around 30 years. The question arises that the natural age of menopause is around 45-55 years, so why is it happening at such an early age? One of the basic reasons is the growing stress level as compared to the old times.

Today, there is a lot of pressure on women to be financially independent. There are different phases of the woman's monthly cycle, which can be categorized as-

- *PUBERTY*- The vast hormonal changes of puberty are severe stressors. A person's body actually CHANGES shape, sexual organs begin to function, and new hormones are released in large quantities. Puberty, as we all know, is very stressful.

- *PRE-MENSTRUAL SYNDROME*- Once a woman passes puberty, her body is designed to function best in the presence of female hormones. For women past puberty, a lack of female hormones is a major stress on the body. Once a month, just prior to menstruation, a woman's hormone levels drop sharply. In many women, the stress of sharply falling hormones is enough to create a temporary OVERSTRESS. This temporary OVERSTRESS is popularly known as **Pre-Menstrual Syndrome (PMS).**

- *POST-PARTUM* -Following a pregnancy, hormone levels CHANGE dramatically. After a normal childbirth or a miscarriage, some women may be thrown into OVERSTRESS by loss of the hormones of pregnancy.

- *MENOPAUSE* -There is another time in a woman's life when hormone levels decline. This is the menopause. The decline in hormones during menopause is slow and steady. Nevertheless, this menopausal decline causes enough stress on the body to produce OVERSTRESS in many women.

On the other hand, the family structure is not as strong as they were, which has put tremendous physical, mental and emotional strain on the women. These pressures, along with the lack of proper nutrition and health awareness, play disastrous effects on the women's health.

Warning Signs of premature menopause
(sometimes same as Natural process)

Physical Signs-
- Irregular periods (change in frequency and duration of periods)
- Infertility
- Hot flashes and Night sweats
- Virginal Dryness
- Bladder control problems
- Insomnia and disturbed sleep
- Palpitations
- Weight gain - around your waist and abdomen
- Skin dryness - dryness and thinning looks
- Headaches
- Breast Tenderness
- Gastric problems

- ❖ Sore joints/Muscles
- ❖ Hair loss and thinning
- ❖ Increase in facial hairs
- ❖ Dry mouth- it is also included with bitter taste and bad breath

Emotional Changes-
- ❖ Irritability
- ❖ Mood swings
- ❖ Lowered sex desires
- ❖ Brain fog- difficulty in concentrations
- ❖ Memory lapses
- ❖ Extreme Tiredness/low energy levels
- ❖ Feeling emotionally detached

Causes-

Apart from the high stress and erratic lifestyle resulting in hormonal imbalance, there are other causes, including genetic factors and cancer treatment along with the STD and TB problems, which can also lead to this problems.

Supportive plans to combat this stress-

Remedies- There is no particular remedy to deal with these great problems but to hit where it starts. It starts from the cause of having unmanageable stress in life. This is also associated with the fast pace of achieving and to forget the value of good and nutritional foods, which is most essential in a working woman. Here are some remedies to deal with this problem in a positive way-

Stress busters Tips -

Due to the extreme stress, the body begins to change its hormonal functions. There is an utmost need to put the mind back into a relaxation phase, which can bring out the happiness desperately needed.

Cinema Therapy- We all know about the cinema, and we hardly know that it can work as a stress-buster. It can be divided into three categories.

- *Evocation Cinema therapy*- The type of movies that help you learn about yourself based on how you respond to different characters.
- *Cathartic Cinema therapy*- Movies help release stuffed-up emotions that can trigger the healing process.
- *Popcorn Cinema therapy*- A feel food therapy, popcorn therapy focuses on how watching films can make you feel better.

This theory is based on the idea that people can identify with certain situations in movies, which can help you either deal with the situations or to detach from them. It can also help you to make a chance to spend your time with yourself and have the complete freedom to choose any type of movie you like; you get a feeling of a sense of achievement and also a break from your daily hectic workload.

Some Diet Suggestions

It is the most important to have a regular balanced diet to overcome this problem-

Some Super Foods you must have-

- *Apple* - High in the Antioxidants, especially in the Peel.
- *Avocado* - Healthy unsaturated fatty acids.
- *Beans* - Low fat healthy protein.
- *Blue berry* - Fruit with most of the Antioxidants.
- *Broccoli* - Best anti-cancer food items.
- *Cinnamon* - One of the oldest spices known for its balanced blood sugar properties.
- *Chocolate* - (Dark) Cocoa is high in Antioxidants and also stress-buster.
- *Dates* - High in Iron, and Potassium.
- *Honey* - Fights Bacteria, Fungus and certain viruses.
- *Kiwi* - Fruit with one of the highest Vitamin C content.
- *Oats* - High in fiber and Proteins, which reduces the chances of heart attacks.
- *Olive Oils* - Healthy unsaturated fatty acids, Vitamin E
- *Onions & Garlic* - High in Flavonoids, Anti-inflammatory
- *Orange* - Vitamin C, Antioxidants
- *Pomegranate* - Antioxidants, Sex Tonic
- *Pumpkin* - High in Carotene.
- *Soya* - This is the most important food to tackle the problems of menopause effects as it contains natural Estrogen, and complete plant protein and anti-cancer properties, which can be used as a natural supplement to the woman's loss of female hormones. It can be a good substitute for the HRT- Hormone Replacement Therapy.
- *Spinach* - Fight heart-related disease, cancer and eye degeneration.
- *Tea* - Green tea has more Flavonoids, antioxidants and protections against some cancer-related aliments in the body.
- *Tomato* - Anti-inflammatory, fights the prostate cancers.
- *Walnut* - Omega-3 fatty acids, Vitamin-E and anti-cancer.
- *Yogurt* - strengthens the Immune system and Digestive system.

- **_Milk_** - Excellent source of Calcium, essential for the prevention of Osteoporosis due to the Menopause stage after stage effects. It also contains -Tryptophan, a chemical that helps the brain ease into sleep mode, that does the trick milk serotonin, So the milk not only prevents you from the Calcium deficiency but also provides you with good sleep.

Problem No 22 – Pregnancy-Related Problems

Stress Builder- Can Stress Effect My Pregnancy Period?

Explanations- Pregnancy is supposed to be a delightful time in our lives, and it can be. This, however, does not mean that it will be without stress. Even wonderful changes can cause stress. Stress is defined as any emotional, mental, or physical changes that can cause a disruption in the normal routine. The effects of stress on the pregnancy, which can be called as- *__Pre-Partum Stress problems__.*

Pre-Partum Stress problems or pregnancy period

Stress comes from both external and internal sources. The phase of the birth of a baby can trigger a range of powerful emotions, such as

- Excitements, joy and even fears. It can also give something which is not expected- Depression.

- Changes in your body, like nausea, vomiting, or fatigue, can affect your daily activities. Interact with your friends and family. This can create stress for you and those around you.

- Will your body cause people to treat you differently? Pregnancy is supposed to be a delightful time in our lives, and it can be. This, however, does not mean that it will be without stress. Even wonderful changes can cause stress.

- Your attitude and thoughts about pregnancy and birth can also cause stress. Will you ever look like you did before pregnancy? Is labor as bad as everyone says? Will you embarrass yourself during the birth? Can you be a good mother? Dads, especially, but moms too, may worry about finances and housing before the baby comes. So, try to relax and do some exercises specially created for stress-free delivery. This will not only ease your mind but also provide a good help in easy delivery.

- Woman who goes through stressful events during the pregnancy periods may be at a greater risk of having an underweight baby, a larger study suggested. A study reported in Psychomatic Medicines, does prove this fact that having a high level of stress hormones in the mother can hinder foetal growth, and severe stress can make it difficult for some pregnant women to follow a healthy lifestyle. The research is based on the findings in the records for the 1.38 million women who gave birth in Denmark between 1979 and 2002.

- Another Study conducted by Bristol University suggests that expectant mothers who feel very anxious have 60% higher chances of having a baby with a problem of Asthma in their later life as compared to the mothers who are more relaxed during the pregnancy period. John Henderson, who led this study, suggests that perhaps the natural response to stress, which produces a variety of hormones in the body may have influences on the developing infant and their developing immune system that manifest themselves later on.

Supportive plans to combat this stress-

During this stage of life, it is the most important to live life in a stress-free atmosphere for the sake of herself along with the development of the baby. I would suggest you a very simple yet effective Stress-buster Exercise, which is highly suitable for the complex body conditions due to the pregnancy.

Art therapy- The next time you feel stressed during the effects of the pregnancy, pick up the paintbrush or pencil and get creative. The American Art Therapy Association believes that making art can help in healing the bad mood. Art Therapy has been extensively researched, and there are therapists who are trained to recognize the nonverbal symbols and metaphors that are communicated within the creative process. This therapy helps people who are going through emotional and mental strains and enables them to express their ideas and thought creativity. Banking on the concept of symbolism and art can be a subtle but effective way to communicate. All you need is some paints and a canvas for your creativity.

Experts Speaks- Art expert says that when you are concentrating on the arts, the alpha brain waves make you more creative. Since it alters the brain wave pattern and distracts you, it makes you more at peace instead of putting your brush away.

Interesting fact- Colors are often representative of feelings and can help in the process of healing. For example, painting with the red color helps you vent your anger, and with the Blue, you can find peace.

Problem No 23 - Early Mother Hood Related Problems

Stress Builder- I Feel Irritated With My New Responsibilities

<u>*Explanations*</u>*-* This is a phase of a woman's life which can turn her whole world upside down. It is also the great stress-filled phase which requires multiple areas to deal with.

Post Partum Stress Problems

There are some of the following symptoms of Post Partum period. A new mother gets affected by these types of depression with the following symptoms-

- Strong feelings of sadness, anxiety or irritability.
- Emotional stress, which interferes with taking care of self and the family.
- Tearfulness.
- Trouble in motivating in normal daily tasks.
- Diminishes interest in food.
- Diminishes interest in Self Grooming.(Dressing, Bathing, Fixing Hair, etc.)
- Inability in sleeping or sleeping too much.
- Trouble in concentrating and making decisions, remembering things.
- Loss of pleasure or interest in the things that used to be fun before.
- Overly intense worry about the Baby.
- Lack of interest in the new baby.
- Fear of harming the baby.
- Thoughts of self-harm or suicide.

Cause of the PPD (Post Partum Stress Problems)

Hormonal Changes-

During the pregnancy, the two female hormones, estrogen and progesterone – in the woman body, increase greatly. In the first 24 hours after the child birth, the amounts of these hormones drop rapidly, and they keep dropping up to a level of before pregnancy level.

Besides the biological changes, there are physical, psychological and environmental factors that can also lead to these problems.

Remedy for curing these problems-

- Get help with cooking, house work and baby care with friends and relatives.
- Sleep when the Baby sleeps.
- Let go of the expectations that you must get everything done.
- Take some time out for yourself and your other family members.
- If your medications make it impossible for you to breastfeed, remember that the good mom is one who takes care of herself so that she could take care of her baby.
- Regular light exercise and proper diet to regain the old figure. It also improves your mood and will give your self esteem a boost as well.
- Do your relaxation exercises, even in a small dose; it can help you relieve enough tension to continue.

Problem No 24 - Menopause Stage Related Stress

Stress Builder- I Am Facing Very Strange Changes In My Body And My Emotional Level. It Is Causing Me A Great Stress. What Should I Do?

<u>Explanation</u> - This is perhaps a complex time in the life of any woman associated with lots of problems on mental as well as physical grounds. It is the time when the hormone level declines fast, resulting in sluggish monthly periods or menopause. It usually occurs at around the age of 51 years, though there are wide variations.

<u>Menopause stage</u> - After pregnancy, the menopause is the strongest biological transitory phase of the woman's life; with menopause, the ovaries stop producing eggs, menstrual activity ceases, and there is a decrease in the production of female hormones - **Estrogen** and **Progesterone** that play the crucial part in the pregnancy and child-bearing. It is the natural process of stoppage of the monthly periods. It is derived from the Greek word "Meno"- Month and the 'Pausis'- Pause.

Decreasing estrogen levels trigger an increase in blood flow to the face, neck, chest and back, thereby the results in hot flashes, mood swings and virginal dryness are also caused by this. Osteoporosis - loss of calcium in the bones causing bone fragility is also common. The risk of heart Disease also increases after menopause as the incidence of cardiovascular risk of high blood pressure and high cholesterol also increases.

Once the level of these hormones dips, a woman's health gets affected by many other problems.

Other symptoms related to this stage-

- Irregular and scanty or heavy Menses.
- Sleeplessness.
- Mood Change.
- Anxiety and Depression
- Irritability and forgetfulness.
- Anger and bitterness.
- Weight Gain.
- Change in Skin.
- Hair Loss.

- Virginal dryness.
- Loss of control of urine.
- Hot Flashes where the lady is sweating even when she is sitting under the Fan.

Menopause can cause-

Cancer of the Cervix-

Weakening of the Bones after menopause or osteoporosis is the most important offshoot. The earlier the menopause, the greater the risk of Osteoporosis. Also, it is more severe in thin women, cigarette smoker women, and sedentary lifestyles.

Supportive plans to combat this stress-

Coping with the Menopause-

Along with dealing with the mental status, there are some medical strategies which can be adopted to overcome this phase of life.

- *__Cancer Screening__*- The important issue of this age group is cancer screening, especially the cancer of the cervix by the PAP smear and Breast cancer check with mammography and sonography. Make sure that the uterus and ovaries are normal. Once the menses stop for one year, the woman should never have any bleeding/discharge again, and if she does, she should meet her gynecologist immediately.

- *__Hot Flashes__* - Hot flashes do not cause any damage and, if mild, can be neglected. Only if it is of a severe nature, they should be treated by certain changes in lifestyle, such as drinking cold liquids, staying in the cool rooms, avoiding going out on the extreme heated days, and avoiding hot flashes triggers, as it can be emotionally and physically, as drinking hot drinks and eating too much spicy foods. Adding some vitamin E and Folic Acids to your diet can help in these conditions.

- *__Hormone Replacement Therapy__*- It involves the giving back the hormones which a woman had in her body prior to the menopause. This is a combination of estrogen and progesterone. However, there are some risks involved in the use of this HRT, which are more in the obese women, smokers, and those who have a family of Breast Cancer. There has been a slight increase in the incidence of strokes and breast cancers in the patients in the long term of HRT therapy. Therefore, there are many alternative drugs available to HRT, which contain the *__Phyto-Estrogens__* or the plant estrogens in the natural forms and much lower doses as for the example of the SOYA; it contains all the necessary elements required for the Menopausal stage, with maximal benefits and minimal side effects.

- *__Regular Exercise__*- A regular exercise will not only help in overcoming the effects of depression and irritability due to menopause, but it will also prevent the risk of Osteoporosis and the related disease, even if it's only for 15 minutes. If you can do it outside, you can do better. Take opportunities like walking up stairs or walking to your local market by walking.

- ***Calm down yourself*-** Get involved in enjoyable activities, such as watching Movies, going on a vacations. It has been seen that visiting a Big Market or a shopping Mall reduces the Stress Hormones in the mind along with lowers your blood pressure, and releases endorphins.

- ***Talk with friends-*** Women are good at making and keeping friends. Building a social support network improves your quality of life and reduces stress over time.

- ***Eat stylishly-*** Do not load up on simple carbohydrates, like sugar that will send your insulin surging. Have lots of vegetables, fruits, and whole grains, and walk away from fatty meals, sodium, alcohol and caffeine.

- ***Have easy workouts*-** Exercise every day, and get off the bus a few blocks from your destination to build walking into your day.

- ***Pamper yourself-*** Do things for yourself that help you relax and feel good. Hot baths, facials, massage or a pedicure remind you that you are important and that your body deserves your attention.

- ***Explore some creative activity-*** Painting, quilting, needlework, acting, or any expressive activity that lets you experience the satisfaction of creating something.

- ***Get spiritual*-** Find a meaningful connection that nourishes your spiritual self. Take spiritual classes of meditations and yoga or some spiritual lessons. It will not only give you relaxation but also keep your stress level down.

- ***Sleep-*** Getting enough sleep is not a waste of time. On the opposing, adequate sleep helps you maintain a healthy weight, sharpens your memory, improves your mood, and increases stamina for facing your busy life.

- ***Learn a stress reduction technique and practice it*-** Meditation, relaxation exercises, mental imagery, deep breathing, or any other technique that you can use during the day to refocus your mind and body away from stress.

- ***Start New Groups-*** Join a group that is dealing with an issue that you are facing. Grief groups, parent groups, divorce support groups, and weight loss groups can support you to get though a challenging time.

- ***Laugh at every opportunity-*** Keeping your life playful and not taking yourself too seriously will reduce your stress and help you roll with life's punches.

- ***Have Regular sex*-** Have satisfying, relaxed sex with your partner. Penetrative sex and orgasm can release chemicals into your system that reduce stress for days.

- ***Get professional Help-*** If you feel you are not managing your stress as well as you'd like, get professional help. You are learning habits to help you live a longer and healthier life. Stress management is not a luxury.

Wherever possible, try to eliminate stressors altogether. And where you can't eliminate them, learn how to manage your response to stressful events and keep them in perspective. Learning stress management will safeguard your health, your sanity and your ability to cope.

Problem No 25 - Headaches Due To Stress

Stress Builder- I Have A Regular Headaches, Is It Due To My Stressful Life?

Explanations - Yes, Of course, having chronic headaches is the most common symptom of the high demands of stressful living. Headaches are a common illness among both sexes, although women do have a slight edge, beating the men out 95% to 90%. Of all the people who suffer from chronic headaches each year, there are a majority of people who suffer from migraines. Migraine headaches occur in women three times as often as in men and affect approximately 18% of women in the United States, while only 6% of men experience migraines. Studies have found clear evidence that 60% of women who experience headaches can trace the root of their headache to their menstrual cycle. Some studies have shown an increased risk of stroke with the use of oral contraceptives.

What causes headaches?

Many people experience different types of headaches at various times, and it is important to get a correct diagnosis of your headache, in which the most common is the Tension Headache. A variety of causes for headaches exist. But they're usually a symptom of an illness, such as a sinus infection, cold, the flu or some other benign illness. But the possibility of a potentially life-threatening illness, such as cerebral hemorrhage, aneurysm, a tumor, or an infection of the brain remains.

Several factors can trigger headaches, including illness, nutrition, and your environment. There are some Foods that can trigger the headaches which are used regularly, such as -

- Chocolate
- Bananas
- Nuts
- Pizza
- Sausage and several junk foods that often trigger migraines
- Excess amounts of coffee, tea, and caffeine Colas may also trigger migraine headaches.

Many patients feel their migraines are the result of allergies from several sources, which are hard to find, as they depend mostly from person to person. Common household chemicals, such as bleach and ammonia, trigger headaches for many people. Others report headaches triggered by things such as perfumes and hair products of different kinds.

Jobs related Headaches-

A new study led by the Queensland University has shown that if one is unhappy with his job, chances are that one can take longer to recover from the back pain than their less stressed friends in the office. According to the researchers, people working in a high-demand but low-control office environments or who have an unhelpful management style at work are most likely to suffer the lower back pain associated with headaches because of the ***Biopsychosocial Factors***. In fact, the Biopsychosocial model, which recognizes the importance of biological, psychological and social factors in illness, is now understood to be central to the understanding of human health in general and pain in particular.

A Practical Example-

Suppose you got up late in the morning and you missed your child's school bus, and you travel all the way to school to drop him off. For this particular incident, your husband gets irritated, and you too got late for your office. At office, you had a very stressful series of events with your clients, and you had arguments with your colleague, and by the time you retire from your office, your bad temper is showing its signs. And by the time you reach your home, you are full with a blowing Headache along with back aches.

You would certainly take OTC painkillers, but the series of stressful events, which has caused this headache will going to last one or two more days without any justified explanation. The main reason behind this type of tiredness and headaches is due to the psychosomatic illness, a kind of tiredness one can feel by the resistance to the events he usually faces every day. For instance- We mostly work as a White-Collar Jobs, but you have noticed that we all are much tired by the evening at the mental as well as Physical levels as compared to the normal blue-collar worker like - Carpenter/Helper, etc.

Headaches can also be a symptom of a more serious disease or infection, which can also be associated with fever or a stiff neck; you should seek immediate medical attention as these are symptoms of meningitis or other serious infections. If your headache is the result of a head injury and lasts more than a few days, it may be serious.

Types and symptoms of headaches

There are three basic types of headaches:

- *Tension*- There are also two types of tension headaches or stress-related Headache. A continuous headache is one which is present when you wake up and all during the day. It is also associated with the Jobs-related pressure and is accompanied with the target oriented jobs.

- *Vascular*- Symptoms of vascular headaches typically include a throbbing pain, which intensifies with physical hard work.

- *Migraine headache*- An aura often precedes a migraine headache, which typically occurs on only one side of the head and often is accompanied by nausea. There are several types of migraine headaches. Symptoms of migraine Headaches include vision disturbance, nausea, vomiting, constipation, and diarrhea. The symptoms may vary from person to person.

What kind of remedies do you have for your headaches?

- Often, keeping a food diary can help you determine if a certain food may be causing your headache.

- Maintaining a regular sleep schedule is helpful in the avoidance of headaches. Too much or too little sleep can contribute to headaches.

- OTC medications are the treatment of choice for most tension headaches. You must follow proper dosing instructions when using any pain medication so that it's not taken too often. Overdose of some OTC medications permanently damages your liver, and overuse of such medications can lead to rebound headaches.

- Biofeedback therapy is many times helpful for reducing headaches and stress by helping you learn to relax.

- Exercise and avoidance of stressful situations and anxiety will often reduce the number of headaches you experience. Walking is a simple exercise that anyone who is ambulatory can do and is a great overall symptom reducer, and it has the added benefit of reducing your risk for many diseases, including heart disease.

- Natural treatments are better than unnatural treatments. Studies have shown that prescription drug use stresses the liver. Some drugs also affect other body organs unfavorably. Though sometimes prescription drug use is necessary, it is wise to seek out alternative approaches when possible.

- Aroma therapy - regular use of certain Aromas can be highly used full in the prevntation of the Headaches, like - Lavender, Eucalyptus, Peppermint, Rosemary etc

- The compression of cold Ice bags can be highly useful in dealing with these problems. Put ice or ice bag behind your neck; it gives you instant relief.

- Record any strange feelings you have before the start of the headache and find how often these symptoms occur. Distinguish between those strange feelings and situations that actually cause you a headache and those feelings that are not. Record all of your "suspicions" and their frequency (stressful events, sleeping difficulties, hormonal factors) to understand what and how they relate to your headaches. Include in your recordings the following information: Date/Time - event/situation (what happened at that time, what have I done, where I was, etc.) - symptoms that caused the headaches - intensity and duration of pain - other accompanying symptoms - Potential "impeller" (e.g. what I had eaten before) - what thoughts did I make.

- Stay calm. Thoughts like "these headaches will never stop", "is terrible, I can not do anything" or "the pain will not let me do anything all day" will not help you cure your headache; on the contrary, they will not let you do anything all day!

- Avoid habits that make headaches more intense. If possible, avoid factors that make headaches more intense. For example, do not drink a lot of coffee, do not stay hungry, etc. Instead, try to overcome your headache by staying relaxed and focused on your activities.

- Avoid further stressful conditions: Do not take extra work, cancel any obligations, and try to relax. Be polite to yourself, as you would be for someone else.

- Do not try to finish everything you have to do before the headache becomes more intense. The objective is to manage the headache, avoid or reduce its intensity, and not be pressed and help it expand.

- Distract your attention away from the pain- Distract your attention from pain. Concentrate for a few minutes on a non-demanding intellectual activity, neutral, repeated, or pleasant. For example, try to remember the lyrics from your favorite song, make in your mind a shopping list, or try to think of something pleasant that will make you happy.

- Self-Massage- The massage in the head, neck, shoulders, and arms is a good method of headache relief. The hypnosis, the placement of ice on the face, a warm bath, and treatment are additional methods that can be used to deal with stress and headaches.

Other factors that can cause a headache-
- Sleep: the long, short or irregular sleep
- Weather Conditions: Changes in temperature or weather conditions
- Strong odors
- High altitude
- Strong lights
- Delay meals or not eating at all
- Dehydration
- Smoking (active or passive)

Headache, most of the times, does not appear immediately but gradually. Usually, we get warnings that start with milder symptoms and gradually weaken. These "headache warnings" may include:

- Nervousness
- Depressed mood
- Tiredness
- Restlessness
- Hyperactivity
- Discomfort from lights, noise and smell
- Stiffness in the neck
- Feeling cold
- Anorexia or severe hunger or intense thirst

After the first appearance of symptoms, a factor that may make the problem worse is the negative way we think about it because when we focus on our physical symptoms; simply, we give them more strength. The way we think about pain and our ability to deal with it may have a definite impact on how to get rid of the headaches. This is because it makes us feel anxiety, depression or anger about our situation, and this leads us to Stressful behaviors.

Remedies for this problem-

- Make sure to have a balanced daily program that will include food, rest and sleep! Do not change your eating habits during the hours and sleep as much as possible.

- Use medications your doctor has recommended to you, do not take larger doses than prescribed, and do not stop medication without your doctor's advice.

- Include relaxing activities in your schedule. Try to do things that make you happy and relaxed.

- Watch your body posture: The tense muscles, like- neck, back, face, and jaw, even the squeak of tightness or teeth due to stress or poor body attitude, tend to increase headaches.

- Locate the stressful factors that dominate your daily life and arrange them in your head: organize your time better, share responsibilities, obligations and feelings with people around you, and tell a heroic "no".

Problem No 26 - Starve To Stress - Slim Forever

Stress Builder- I Wish To Have A Slim Figure, I Am Deeply Stressed To Get It. What Should I Do?

<u>Explanation-</u> This is what most of the teenage girls want to be these days. Slim forever – this is the most common thing seen to be developing in the modern world, which exceeds the disorder called the Anorexia Nervosa or self starving. The ideal image of a woman's body has changed radically in the past few years. Many Teenage girls and, in fact, several grown-up women struggle to feel good about their bodies. They tend to compare themselves to the glamorous models of the fashion magazines and hoardings without realizing the real facts about their bodies.

Anorexia Nervosa is an eating disorder centered on an excessive fear of weight gain. Around 95% of the people who are affected by this problem are the female, but some males can also develop this problem.

Causes-

- Psychological factors, such as the fear of sexuality at this age. Past negative experiences and perceived loss of control can lead to this problem.
- Females that are over-protective or focused on the achievement can produce an Anorexic member in the family.
- Constantly criticizing one for his own body and appearance, combined with low esteem.
- Societal pressure to look and behave in a certain manner at the adolescent.
- Certain personality traits like perfectionism, approval-seeking behavior and obsessiveness are associated with this disorder.
- There is a possibility of hereditary re-disposition that usually becomes noticeable at the time of puberty.

Symptoms related to this disorder-

- Excessive Dieting, exercising usually beyond the justified reasonable control.
- Significant weight loss without any solid reason.
- Self-prescription for the medicines that reduce weight, without any recommendations.
- Avoid any social gathering where any food is involved.

- Weighing yourself several times in a day and stressing yourself on the slightest of changes.
- Misuse of Laxatives, diuretics and enemas.
- Decrease in the attention spans and concentrations.
- Developing food rituals that allow for eating very little, eating in the sacristy, eating in certain orders, and excess chewing.
- Disturbed sleep leads to fatigue and tiredness, which can lead to fainting in the daytime.

Effects-
- Girls may experience loss of menstrual cycle (***Amenorrhea***) and disturbance, which can lead to not only in fertility but also in bone density growth.
- Muscles loss and weakness.
- Lowered body resistance to fight disease.
- Digestive problems such as constipation.
- Severe dehydration, which can lead to kidney failure.
- Feeling of guilt and depression.
- Isolation from the friends circle.
- Brittle nails and hair.
- Dry and yellow skin.
- Mild anemia, swollen joints.
- Changes in the kidney functions which lead to the potassium deficiency, and increased or decreased urination.

Supportive plans to combat this stress-
- Rather than comparing with anyone, one should be happy as the way he is; every one is unique in every sense. It may be a very strong possibility that a person may not be good-looking but the intelligence and the knowledge he possesses is extraordinary. So, rather than looking for the external beauty, the inner beauty and knowledge are much more important. You can check the history; the most famous and the most powerful people never have good-looking features, yet they rule the world with their personalities.
- It is the duty of the family members to help the person suffering from this problem. Rather than criticizing, and the comparing, they should expect the facts and try to help the person with help and counselling.
- Try to motivate the person for living a normal life and accompany him to family celebrations.

- Try to share the foods with him so that he shall realize what he /she has been missing.
- The primary goal is to achieve the normal health for the person, which may involve the hospitalization or the professional help in the mode of behavior therapy, family therapy etc.

Problem No 27 - Skin Problems Due To Stress

Stress Builder- I Am Facing Regular Skin Problems, Is It Relate To Stress?

Explanations- Yes, of course, it is deeply related to unmanaged stress and its effects.

Stress increases the level of toxicity in the body and contributes to hormonal imbalances, both of which have effects on the skin. It can make the dry skin drier and the oily skin oilier. The visible effects on the skin include-

- Acne
- Spots
- Eczema
- Psoriasis
- Excessive Pallor
- Skin disease and many more complications

The recent studies conducted in this regard to prove the relationship, but also to provide a possible explanation. The study, conducted by researchers at Wake Forest, followed 94 high school students with mild or moderate Acne for the several months. Acne is generally associated with a high level of sebum, the oily substance that coats the skin and protects the hair because the sebum levels are known to wax and wane with variations in weather; the study was conducted where the temperature and humidity rarely change, in Singapore.

Using the standard measure of stress, the researchers showed that in periods of high emotional stress, like before the exams, the students were 23% more likely to experience breakouts. At the same time, the sebum productions did not vary much, whether they were experiencing high or low stress, indicating that levels of the substance had little or no role. Instead, the result may have more to do with inflammation. Other studies have shown that stress can provoke inflammation, and acne is an inflammatory disease.

Most women experience hormonal imbalance when they are in their premenstrual stages or when having their periods. The main outcome of hormonal imbalance in this age group is the Acne.

Estrogen and testosterone imbalances occur easily and can be caused by the stress levels and certain types of medications. Hormone imbalance leads to an overproduction of sebum, an oily secretion of the skin; it closes up the pores, causing both Blackheads and Whiteheads.

Besides the Acne, those women who suffer from polycystic ovaries manifest symptoms, like dark skin patches on the neck, groin, and underarms, as well as skin folds or skin tags in the armpits or the neck area.

The Menopausal Women- There are also great effects on the skin during the menopause stage of women. Estrogen controls the moisture and the oil balance, and therefore, with depleting levels of estrogen – due to the Menopause, the skin starts to get dry, and the first sign is fine lines and wrinkles appear. Other symptoms include poor blood circulation and lowering of immunity, causing the skin to erupt into allergies easily.

5 signs that you are stressed-

- You have become clumsy. Stress affects coordination, making you drop things or bump into the furniture more than usual.
- You are forgetful-leaving shops without taking your change suggests that you are too frantic to focus on the here and now.
- You constantly crave sugary or fatty foods-stress uses up a lot of energy, so when you are under pressure, you can crave a quick fix
- Your temper is frayed-exploding over the smallest things is making your nerves shredded, and you need to recharge.
- You are always ill-stressed, which suppresses the immune system, leaving you to susceptible to cough, colds and fever.

Supportive plans to combat this stress-

Tips to have beautiful skin-

- Have vegetables, fruit and whole grains. They are full of fibers that help in flushing out harmful toxins, along with Vitamin B, which helps in regulating metabolic functions.
- Including citrus fruits like oranges, lime, guava, grapefruits, and Amla, Indian gooseberry. They are full of Vitamin C needed for the formations of collagen, which gives elasticity to the skin.
- Include nuts and seeds, raw and roasted; they prevent damage to both external and internal factors.
- Do not forget to take the flax seeds, apple, leafy vegetables and omega-3 fatty acids for shiny skin.
- Drink around 8-10 full glasses of water.

Exercise to Reduce Stress Effects on Skin-

- Yoga is very useful for the prevantation of skin-related disorders related to stress-
- Sarvanga Asan
- Shrish Asan

- Yog Mudras
- Singhasan
- meditations

Do exercise regularly; it can benefit the skin.

Other suggestions for the skin-
- Sweating is a must as it flashes out the toxins, so do not forget to indulge in some vigorous exercises, like running and brisk walking. Also, steam sauna can also be useful to flush out the excess toxins from the body and to regenerate your skin.

Precautions- If you are suffering from high B.P. or any other aliment, kindly see your medical consultant before starting these sweating exercises.

Problem No 28 - Nails Problems Due To Stressful Life

Stress Builder - I Have A Problem Of Broken Nails. Is It Due To Stress full life?

Explanations- Felling stressed due to Broken Nails and Brittle Hair. There is an explanation, which is related to stressful living, as they are the external indicators. While everyone knows that stress can take a toll on a person psychologically, researchers in the United States have carried out a study and found that it also can lead to dermatological problems, like acne, Brittle nails and hair loss. The Science Daily reported that –When a person becomes stressed, the level of the body's stress hormone –Cortisol rises, which in turn can increase the oil production, which can lead to oily skin and other beauty problems. This research was conducted by Dr. Flor, A Mayoral of the University of Miami's Miller School of Medicine. Dr. Mayoral and his fellow researchers came to a conclusion after the analyzing a study of 27 medical and Pharmacy students.

Nails also reflect the status of your health. If you are not fit internally, it clearly shows its signs on the Nails, such as-

- Brittle nails are caused by the lack of proper amount of water in the body. Ironically, prolonged exposure of nails to water also causes this, as do certain health conditions; symptoms include easy peeling at the nail edge, breakage and layering.
- Discolored nails are due to anemia, a common problem among women.
- Blue nails are the indications of certain heart and liver diseases.
- White spots in the nails are formed when there is low blood supply to the nails. They could be a result of injury and internal disease.
- Pain and swelling in and around the nails can be indications of fungal infections.
- Thickened; this may be due to psoriasis or fungal infection.
- Splitting, usually due to nails being exposed to certain chemicals, repeated wet and dry conditions.
- Dull color and brittle nails can be due to vitamin deficiency.

Supportive plans to combat this stress-

Remedy for the Stressed nails-
- Wearing rubber gloves for the protection of the nails while doing any rough jobs is the best remedy for the nails.
- Never peeling or scraping nail polish from the nails.
- Stop biting your nails in the stressful event will certainly help.
- Keeping the nails short and shaped with rounded tips, if you regularly engage in the activities, like sports, jobs, etc.
- Do not use your nail as a tool - No picking, No picking, No Digging, etc.
- Try to keep your hands dry and moisturized.

Diet for beautiful Nails-
- Biotin is essential for the nails. Have foods, like Soya and whole grains that are rich in Biotin.
- Your diet must include fruits and vegetables to supply necessary vitamins, minerals and enzymes required for beautiful nails.
- Consume adequate fluids.
- A glass of carrot juice every day provides necessary calcium and phosphorus for nails.

Simple tips for Nail Care
- Soak your hands in Luke warm water for 10 minutes everyday, preferably before sleeping; it will not only distress your hands ,but also give you beautiful hands and nails.
- Apply creams and lotions whenever you wash your hands with soaps.
- Do not wear tight shoes as they may damage your toe nails.
- If you wear the closed shoes, clip your toenails first short to avoid any damage to the toenails.
- To whiten the nails, use whitening toothpaste. Scrub your nails to de-stain and add sparkle.
- Soak your nails in lemon juice and water. The lemon acts as an astringent and lifts the strain from the nails.
- Light massage with Olive Oils can do wonders for the tired nails.

Emotional Problems Due To Stress

Problem No 29 - Negative Thoughts

Stress Builder- I Can't Stop My Mind Thinking About The Unexpected

Explanations- As in the first chapter about the types of stress, I have clearly mentioned about the Imaginary stress, the type of stress which haunts our mind and builds our perceptions of life and to deal with others. This process is unstoppable and continues to perform throughout the day, the unimaginable events haunt the mind, and even if we try to stop them, but we can't. The best thing about this type of problem is that from the outside, there are hardly any visible signs of the problems or the strain which we are facing, but from the inside, you will be surprised to know that imaginary stress is as dangerous as the real stress. There is one more surprise for you; it has been found that this type of stress is highly available in the female counterparts as compared to the males. This is because of the conservative nature and less freedom of expression of views available to them.

In practice, we see that lots of the things in our daily events are concerned and highly affected by imaginary stress. If someone imagines that his husband is having some extramarital affair in his office, even if his husband proves and confirms his best, the attitude remains the same, and it not only affects the wife's health but can also create a disaster for his husband. In this fast world, we always have the nature of we believe what we see. Most of the time, it proves to be wrong about the belief we have created in the mind. I have heard a very interesting short story about this particular problem. You will find what kind of problems can be created when our minds resolve to a certain problem which will never happen-

Imaginary Stress-

In the olden days, in rural areas, a man was going to another village on a bicycle. The weather was quite hot, and after traveling for several hours, the man finally got thirsty and tired. He found a large house on the road and decided to take some rest there. In the old days, it was quite common to expect some help from anyone as people are quite helpful by nature.

The man reached the big house, parked his bicycle in the courtyard, and sat down under the tree. The house owner lady was doing some home works and welcomed him. She also asked her daughter-in-law to get some water for the man. The man was quite happy with their behavior and waited for the water.

The daughter-in-law went inside the house to get some water from the pot and noticed that an axe was hanging above the water pot. Her mind quickly resolved into the

imaginary stress, and she began to think that if his son would have come to fetch the water from the pot and, if by chance, the axe fell upon him, he would have been killed. On imagining this extreme thing, she began to make lots of hues and cries, as her son would have actually been killed in the accident.

When her crying voice reached outside, her mother-in-law rushed inside, and when she enquired that the son had been killed, she also began to cry.

The man sitting outside hear the voice, and before he could understand anything, the other family members also joined that Scene; meanwhile, the neighbors also assembled in the house, and they also began to cry.

The man, who was waiting for the water, thought that there might be a great accident happening inside the house, and finally, he thought to enquire about the incident and went inside the house.

When he entered the house, he saw everyone was crying. When he asked for the reason for crying from the daughter-in-law, she said that her son had been killed by the fallen axe. To his great surprise, he found nothing tragic, so he asked again that – where is the son? Now, the mother-in-law got angry with him and said – What a fool you are! Don't you look that she is newly wed to this house? How is it possible to have a son so soon? And she began to cry again. That man was deeply shocked. He had never seen a group of stupid people who were just crying in the extremes of Imaginary stress upon a matter that was too far to be happened in practical.

He quickly came out of this house, took his bicycle and ran away from the house.

This little story shows what happens when we use our minds in extremes in imaginary stress. If we calculate our perceptions, we find that there are chances of hearing or seeing the things, which may not be fair, but later we came to know that most of the time our perception is wrong.

You must have seen that if we take any problem and think about all the possible aspects to deal with it in the morning, we find it hard to get sleep with it, and when confronted with that practical problem in the morning, we are certainly surprised to see that the problems usually come along with the easiest solutions with itself. The solution that is the easiest and the most unimaginable to our minds.

When someone is a rationalist and does everything based on just cold calculations and logic, one is likely to make mistakes because of a lack of sensitivity. One cannot understand how cruel and cold he or she is - the person believes that the way he or she thinks is absolutely correct and that he or she is right in considering only logic and disregarding feelings and emotions. One may have the intuition urging him or her to consider emotions and feelings; however, the intuition may not be strong enough.

When people want to be silent the straight away result is the opposite; when the body is still, the mind starts working like a machine, and in spite of all our efforts, we cannot stop this function for the better harmony between our thoughts and our body. I suggest you do a simple exercise to take control of your mind.

Supportive plans to combat this stress-

We all know that breathing is the first thing which gets affected by our negative thoughts. So, if we control the breathing cycle along with our thoughts, the problems of unnecessary thinking can be cured, therefore, I suggest Walk Therapy for this purpose-

Walk Therapy-

Walking not only gives you an overhaul of your sense of well-being, but it can also cure many problems at the mental and the physical levels. Walking gives you a shot of natural morphine, an endorphin which is responsible for the feel-good effect you experience every time you walk in a positive state of mind and helps you think clearly. It is also an alternative form of medicine, which increases the heart rate and skin response, such as sweating, which in turn sends neurotransmitters to the brain. In order to get a better concentration on the feelings, one should concentrate on the breathing cycle. By concentrating on the breathing one can control the imaginary thoughts, which come into the mind automatically as the mind remains vacant. This exercise is highly useful in controlling the negative thoughts, and the person is more aware of internal activities like heartbeats, which are as good as meditation as they claim the mind completely.

Interesting fact- One of the cheapest and the economical ways to get rid of the unwanted thoughts, this works like an antidepressant. Walking is now being described as one of the best **Ecotherepies** too. It had been categorized as a therapy back in 1970s when a book titled -**Conquering Depressions and Anxiety through Exercise** was published.

Problem No 30 - Eating Problems Related To Stress

Stress Builder- I Can Not Control Eating When I Am Stressed

Explanations- Stress and eating are highly coordinated. What is the single most common problem people faced when they want to lose the weight? It is the Emotional Eating. It is the state of mind that whenever one feels stressed, one starts eating without the consent about the quality of food or the quantity required for the body. The reason behind this is based on the type of stress and the stress hormone level that affects the body.

Other factures behind these problems are-
- *Cortisol Cravings*: Stress can bring on increased levels of Cortisol, known as "the stress hormone." Cortisol has a beneficial function in the body, but excessive levels of Cortisol can create problems in the body. Among other things, high levels of Cortisol can create cravings for salty and sweet foods. In previous centuries, this enabled people to bulk up on foods that would sustain them during times when food is scarce; however, in modern times and industrialized nations, when food is rarely scarce, this previously adaptive mechanism causes excess weight gain.
- *Social Eating:* Often, people who are under stress will seek out social support, which is a great way to relieve stress. Unfortunately for dieters, when people get together - especially women - we tend to go out for a nice meal. Crying on your friend's shoulder over a couple of meals, full of high fats or sharing a bowl of chips with the guys as you watch a T.V. serials are all social forms of emotional eating. It can make you feel better in the short term, but you may regret it later as it can create a lot of problems.
- *Nervous Energy*: When stressed or anxious, many people become "orally restless." Sometimes, this leads to nail biting or teeth grinding, and often, it leads to eating when not hungry. Many people, out of nervousness or boredom, just munch on chips or drink colas to give their mouths something to do.
- *Childhood Habits:* Many of us have comforting childhood memories that revolve around food. Whether your parents used to reward you with sweets or with an ice cream cone, in times of stress, few things can be as powerfully comforting or rewarding as your favorite food. Because many people don't develop more effective coping strategies, this type of Emotional eating is very common: people eat to celebrate, eat to feel better, and eat to deal with the stress of being overweight.
- *Stuffing Emotions*: People who are uncomfortable with confrontation may deal with frustrations in their marriage with a piece of cake, for example, rather than with open communication. Food can take the focus off of anger, resentment, fear, anxiety, and a

host of other emotions. We may not be aware of the facts, but we often use the foods for this purpose.

What we do when we go for the Emotional Eating-

- *Drinking Too Much Tea/Coffee*: When we live life under heavy stress, people often find themselves using coffee drinks to jump-start themselves in the morning and a pattern of all-day coffee drinking.

- *Eating the Wrong Foods*: Due partially to increase the levels of Cortisol, the stress hormone, stressed people tend to crave foods high in fat, sugar and salt. This gives them some sort of energy and relaxation.

- *Skipping Meals*: Another thing overly stressed people tend to do is skip meals. Have you ever found yourself rushing out of the house without a healthy breakfast or realizing you're starving in the late afternoon because you didn't eat enough? It is because, in the events of stress, we tend to forget the basic requirements of the body.

- *Mindless Munching*: Conversely, stress also makes us prone to emotional eating, when we eat when we aren't hungry or eat foods that are bad for us. Have you found yourself mindlessly snacking on junk food or eating when you aren't hungry because of stress? In fact, a lot of people are carrying a packet of chips in their bags for their daily dose.

- *Forgetting Water*: With busy lives, it's easy to forget to drink your water; in fact, a good portion of people drink no water and get water only from colas or coffee. Do you get a full eight glasses per day, or even four? Because we believe that having colas or coffee can be a substitute for water.

- *Fast Food*: People these days eat at home less than in generations past, as it's easier to just drive through a fast food place or go to a restaurant than to go home and cook something. Unfortunately, this gets expensive and is often unhealthy.

- *Crash Diets*: Because of weight gain from stress, some people intentionally eat less food than they need or try dangerous fad diets in order to lose the excess weight. Diets that aren't balanced with fruits and vegetables, protein and healthy carbohydrates can often be bad for your health in the long run, even if they look attractive in the short term.

These unhealthy habits can affect our bodies in many ways. The following are only some of them:

- *Blood Sugar Imbalances*: When we don't eat enough food or don't eat healthy enough food (too little protein and healthy carbohydrates, too much sugar, etc.), we can experience blood sugar fluctuations. These fluctuations can lead to mood swings, fatigue, poor concentration and other negative consequences in the short term, and greater health problems like hyperglycemia in the long run.

- *Caffeine Side Effects*: Too much caffeine can lead to poor concentration and decreased effectiveness, sleep disturbances, and increased levels of Cortisol in the blood, as well as other negative effects.

- ***Poor Health Outcomes***: Poor nutrition can also lead to lowered immunity, so you're more susceptible to illnesses: both minor and major. As you can imagine, this can lead to other problems, including increased stress levels, and it can also have great effects on the Monthly cycles.

Supportive plans to combat this stress-

Fortunately, there are many proactive steps which can be used to deal with these problems. These steps range wildly from basic relaxation techniques to the development of a reliable support network, and other options are included as follows-

- Keeping a food journal/ Diary to help identify the emotional eating triggers.
- Cultivating mental and emotional well-being through practice, like Meditation, mindfulness, massage and Yoga.
- Develop good problem-solving skills.

Here is a good exercise which can prevent you from emotional eating-

- Take a deep breathe and count from 1 to 10 in reverse mode. If stressful situations involve someone else, take a time out and agree to continue after a few minutes.
- Remind yourself where you are. Take a look around, and noticing and remembering the names and the colors of the things around you will distract your mind for a few minutes.
- Now, try to gain control and, if possible, drink a glass of water; this will not only help you in getting control over your thoughts but also give some soothing effects.

The main idea is to stay in your body and in the moment,- with what is real, instead of going inside and munching whatever you find and getting out of control .

Cope in Healthy Ways

Many people use food to deal with uncomfortable emotions like anger, frustration, fear, and other feelings. While we need food for survival, there are healthier ways to cope with emotions:

- ***Talk To A Friend-*** Social support can go a long way toward helping you process your feelings, gain support if needed, and move on.
- ***Try Journaling-*** Processing one's feelings in a journal has been found to have many health benefits beyond mere stress management. When you feel like reaching unhealthy food, reach a pen, instead.
- ***Exercise-*** Getting your body moving is a great way to blow off steam and get your endorphins going, and it is a much healthier option than overeating.
- ***Face Your Problems-*** If you're using food to soften your feelings in a difficult relationship, try boldness instead. If food is your only treat at a job you hate, try techniques for finding satisfaction at your job, or get a different one. Cut down on the stress and you won't need food to help you cope.

- ***Try Healthy Alternatives-*** If these techniques don't completely eliminate your emotional eating urges, go ahead and indulge, but use healthier fare. Drink fresh fruit juice instead of colas; munch on veggies or healthy snacks instead of chips; savor one small piece of dark chocolate instead of binging on a whole chocolate muffin. All of these things can be good for you, so you'll still come out ahead without feeling completely disadvantaged.

Problem No 31- Worrying Too Much

Stress Builder - I Keep On Worrying About The Unnecessary Topics This Gives Me Unnecessary Stress

Explanations- Worrying about the future or the common conditions of the state is a normal affair. Security about the terror and economy may be our first concern today but excessive worrying about these problems is some sort of emotional imbalance which can create a lot of stress and problems for the person himself as well as the person around him. It is a common to wake up in the 3 A.M., and you're awake with palms sweaty, your mind racing and worried about your life, your kids, your professions and your parents, your promotions and what people are thinking about you.

These are the common sight in today's life. The more you are successful, the more of this problem you are facing - you hear about the Robbery or the murder next block, and you have the extreme stress of your life. You resemble all the incidents similar to your life and start living in the panic and worrying about the unexpected in your life. You become over cautious, which not only changes the way you live but also creates many health problems in the long run.

Top worries are the health, money, relations, crime, the high cost of living, terrorism and the future of your child. A teenager worries about her mom, his secret belongings, and a little school girl even worries about her dog's health.

The worry chart of an average man-

- 80% of the people worry about the Family matters.
- 75% of people worry about the Relationships Matters.
- 60% worry about the Health.
- 50% worry about the small things.
- 50% worry about - ifs.
- And a small group of people worry about not having any significant topic to worry about.

Worry is a state of mind, which resolves a particular matter without any proper justification. Because of the complex mind, women are more prone to these problems as compared to the men. Some more equations for the worrying.

What do women fear?
- 85% panic about the office politics.
- 79% fear about the relationships - marriage, sex and betrayal.
- 68% panic and worry about not being liked enough.
- 50% worry about the household jobs, maid servant going on leave.
- 78% women worry about if they put on weight.

What do Men Fear?
- 80% men fear about accident
- 80.5% worry about their jobs and finances.
- 79% worry about their sexual performances.
- 65% worry about paying bills on time.
- 70% worry about being laughed at.
- 50% worry about loneliness.

What do children worry about?
- 80% worry about losing friends.
- 90% worry about the doing badly in exams.
- 50% worry about being laughed or Bullied
- 75% girls worried about to make good impressions.

Supportive plans to combat this stress-

The habit of worrying is difficult to stop. There are a few psychological tips to tackle this horrible habit.

- There is a useful remedy to deal with this problem if you simply cultivate your habits of postponing worrying. Your mind become reconditioned not to dwell on worries in the present. The trick is that whenever you feel overwhelmed by notions of worrying thoughts, note them on the piece of paper and keep or mention a date to focus on this issue; your mind is so powerful that you instantly start to consider other current issues rather than this one. You can forget about it, knowing that you plan to worry about it later aside for its purpose- you can forget about it, knowing that you plan to worry about it later.

- Optimistic approach helps- Practice positive approach by thinking about the time when you were relaxed and at peace. Try to relocate the situations against your mind, thinking about the sights, sound, and smell you experience through the Guided imaginary Exercise. You will find that after the exercise of 10-15 minutes, you will feel instance relief. Some people call it as day-dreaming, but it is a very effective tool to deal with imaginary stress.

- Introspect often- Take time out for yourself. Keep yourself busy. You deserve to take a break occasionally and do not feel guilty about it. Accept your weakness and your strength, and if you do not like yourself, you can not expect anyone else to do the same.

Problem No 32 - Adjustment Disorder

Stress Builder- It Is Really Hard For Me To Adjust With My Family Members, I Really Feel Stressed About It?

Explanations- It is quite common problems among the people who have faced stress from their family background. It is an extreme reaction to an individual life stressor. The reaction is ruthless compared with what would normally be expected and can result in significant destruction in social, occupational or academic functioning. The response may be associated with a single event, like an Accidents, a Poor marriage relations, divorce, or a new job in a remote area. It can also be associated with many events like severe business difficulties and inhabiting down on an unknown area. It can also made to some extent by the family problems, like witnessing parents constantly fighting, chemotherapy, and Extreme financial difficulties.

Adjustment Disorder often occurs with one of the following:

- Depressed mood (patient is tearful, sad, hopeless); anxiety (patient is nervous, fearful, worried)
- Mixed disturbance of emotions and conduct physical complaints, social isolation. weaken occupational/social functioning
- Physical complaints (e.g. general aches and pains, stomachache, headache, chest pain), palpitations conduct disturbances, withdrawal from daily activities.

Note: Symptoms may vary widely.

There is no way to predict which people are likely to develop adjustment disorder, given the same stressor. Factors that influence how well a person reacts to stress may include economic conditions, availability of social support, and occupational and recreational opportunities. Intrapersonal susceptibility to stress may include such factors as social skills, intelligence, genetics and coping strategies.

Supportive plans to combat this stress-

The main focus for this type of stress-related problems is to relieve indication and help the person achieve a level of functioning comparable to that before the stressful event.

- It includes individual psychotherapy, family therapy, and behavior therapy. Rather than expecting a quick response, short-term goals are expected, as the course of adjustment disorder is short-term in nature.

- A relaxation technique proves to be helping the person deal with feelings of stress. This includes **the Meditations, Walk therapy, Aromatherapy and Art therapy,** which can help him in expressing his feelings, and in long run, can make his mind stress free.

- In this particular type of stress, a person often feels that he is quite alone, and a sense of insecurity overwhelms his mind. He may become overprotective and defensive by nature. In the events of events of extreme stress, a person may think about suicide or harming himself in any manner to gain sympathy from others.

To overcome this problem, the easiest way I suggest a simple yet effective therapy to overcome this problem-

- *The Hug Therapy*- Mata Amrita Anandmayyi Devi has catapulted this therapy to fame, and today, it is recognized as a worldwide treatment – It has been known as the transformation of positive Vibes. Scientific research has proved that the sense of touch is always healing; it can help in relieving pain and can even fight bouts of anxiety. The power of love can make a great difference to those who are going through a troubled time and extreme mental stress. It does not matter by whom who gets a hug, the therapeutic touch can bring the physiological changes to a person; just as a children are comforted by the hugs of their parents, adults are also reassured when enveloped in the warmth of an embracement. So, next time, if you feel too much depressed and lonely, go ahead and hug your friend or relative.

- *Experts says* - It has been based on the power of love. It starts with a series of positive emotions. It is especially beneficial for those who are going through a sense of loss and sadness, which leads to an adjustments in relations.

- *Interesting Facts*- Kathleen Keating, US-based Hug expert has authored a book titles **The hug Therapy Book**. She talks about how hugging accomplished many things, such as physical fitness- as it keeps arms and shoulder in good condition, a great sense of self esteem and high emotional awareness.

I had a lady patient some time ago whose family members are very much disturbed because of her behavior. As she got up from the bed in the morning, she looked highly depressed and began to cry by the slightest provocations. When I asked the lady about her behavior towards the family member, she told me that as soon as she got up in the morning, her mind resolveed to the unnecessary matters, and she found herself in the middle of the extreme stress. She knew that she was not doing well for her family, but she was helpless as her mind ran after the problems. The problems were strange but due to the imaginary stress, people found themselves having the adjustment problems, in spite of their good and harmless nature.

I found a very unique way to deal with this particular type of problem with this lady.

I asked her son to purchase an iPod and fill it with the spiritual bhanjans and asked the lady to use it as soon as she got up from the bed, Put the speakers of iPod in her ears and do all her daily activities as usual.

I was really surprised to hear from his son that the idea worked wonderfully. Due to the imaginary stress, her mind constantly resolved into stupid matters, and when she used the iPod, the music immediately stopped that process, and she began to live in more relaxed way, and it was more relaxed for her family members also. Others suggestions are:

__Communication gaps__- Listen patiently. Also, try to understand what your spouse is saying. Avoid smashing those ideas even if you think the person is in the wrong. Save the criticism for later. Tell the person everything you feel. To expect your partner to understand everything without being told is expecting too much.

__Give space to Live-__ Made-for-each-other, which doesn't involve binding each other. You are two different people who need some personal space to develop as individuals. Not only will it keep both enthusiastic, but it will also provide you with a lot more to keep your marriage.

__Fight but in a fair manner__- Fight your battle with your partner. It will only clear things up. But make it fair. Trying to win a fight is not the solution. The idea should be to curb your anger and solve differences without letting arguments go out of control. Do not forget to throw the egos out of the window.

__Avoid conquering your partner-__ The husband can cook, and the woman can earn. Just because you are married, you don't have to get caught up in a daily routine of being husband and wife. It is a partnership, not ownership.

__Be practical__- What you thought was endearing about your spouse when you were only dating is probably the reason you are fighting. Or you have discovered things about the person you think you would rather scoot for hell than witness. Learn to work around them because expecting perfection from anyone is unrealistic and can get too demanding.

__Think positive about your relations__- There are all sort of problems to every warm relationship. What you need to do is look at those positive aspects of your relationship that can further strengthen your marriage. At the same time, work on your weaker points, so they don't surface too often.

__Understanding-__ Do not try to use 'you said' and 'you did'. Look within and try putting yourself in the shoes of your partner. It will give you a whole new viewpoint that you might need to work on even if it means sacrificing your preferences.

__Recognize-__ If you think fighting over his alcoholism is the way out, you need a shift of standard. Accepting the person for who he or she is more likely to change the person, lending safety measures and belief to your love.

Adjustment disorder is defined as beginning within three months of the beginning of a certain stressor and lasting no longer than six months after the stressors have ceased. Most people recover from adjustment disorders without any remaining symptoms if they have no previous history of mental illness and have access to constant social support.

It is important for these individuals to maintain and develop healthy diets and sleeping patterns as well as develop and maintain strong social support.

Problem No 33 - Self harming Attitude

Stress builder- Is my own attitude harming my well-being?

Explanations- Of course, your own attitude does more harm to you than anybody else in the world. We often hear that **It is all in the Mind**- Every problem originates as a thought in the mind before manifesting itself first emotionally, and then physically. For example, if any of your beloved friends die of a heart attack, you will find the same symptoms in yourself, and you can even admitted to the hospital with chest pain. Even though all the medical reports were normal, you will remain live in the fear of dying by the a heart attack. In my medical career, I have seen many patients admitted to the hospital, complaining about severe problems, yet they are normal, and after paying heavy consultation charges to the hospital, they feel better. The most sought-after trouble one can see is the fear of death. Whenever one hears the death of anybody, he shows the same body signs and thinks that he is the next. The main problem is not far away but lies deep inside of his brain.

Here is the list of some of these harmful attitude, which you do to you self. You will find out that all your all problems are called "YOU".

Take this simple Quiz, and if you answer YES to any of the questions, you might be suffering from your self-thoughts-

Questions Box-

- No matter how much you earn, money always remains a major issue for you.
- You can not lose your weight, no matter how hard you try.
- You are an alcoholic, Smoker or Drug addict. You know that you should quit, but in spite of all your efforts, you just cannot.
- Your spouse is your Punching bag, and you relieve your stress through it.
- You blank out before an examination or any important meeting.
- You always criticize your partner in the anticipation of being dumped.
- Your mood usually swings between too happy or too sad.

Supportive plans to combat this stress-

These are quite common in the fast pace of life; we often look for the magical potion that keeps us happy forever and also away from all fear and provides us with the ultimate health. Since it is not possible, you might want to try some alternative therapies that can lift your mood and keep you cheerful. However, do not expect to have overnight results - practice these therapies and boast of a pleasant disposition forever-

- Whenever you feel the dip in mood, just go for the Shava Asans pose; try to concentrate and be rooted in the present. Chant cheers, full suggestions like Be Happy or be tension-free, prefer to use one word instead of the sentence as it triggers the required emotions faster. In about 3-4 minutes, you will feel the difference. If you are in the office or traveling, try to do this in a comfortable position. You will wipe out all the negative emotions along with feeling low or irritated. I prefer Shavaasana because in this position, you are the most connected with the earth, whereby its gravity absorbs all the stress, and you become relaxed. Therefore you will feel much better.

- Sujok therapy- A modified version of the Acupuncture, Su-Jok has been introduced by the Korean professor, Park Jae Woo. According to Woo, each body part is represented by the hands and feet; for instance, the thumb represents the head and neck. There are certain energy points on these organs, on which when the pressure is applied, relief is applied to the affected body part. The therapy balance the energy in the tissue, dells and organs, thereby provide the relief. It is quite effective and mood enhancement. But there is one precaution for using this therapy: the complete knowledge of the energy points is essential, and the accurate bearable pressure should be applied.

- It has been observed that most of the women in urban as well as in the rural areas are careless about their medical evolution needs every year due to the attitude or the tendency to surrender to the growing stress level in their personal lives. This will not cause a greater risk to the unknown disease lying under the skin, but it can be a highly stressful event in the future. Therefore it is highly recommended to have a thorough medical check up every year.

- ***Three Rules to cure your overstress-*** There are basically three rules you should follow when you feel that you are overstressed. These are simple and provide an instant relief.

Rule -1- Learn to read your body signs.

Learn to check your body frequently for signs of OVERSTRESS. Watch for the revealing disturbances in your sleep pattern, as this is usually the earliest sign of OVERSTRESS. You must learn to read your body signs in much the same way as the diabetic learns the early warning signs of abnormal blood sugar. In order to cope successfully with diabetes, the diabetic has to learn to read his body's signals. If he has a constant thirst, fatigue and excessive urination, that means his sugar is too high. If he has shakiness, irritability, and perspiration that means the blood sugar is too low. In order to live with diabetes, the diabetic must understand what these signals mean. Likewise, if you are a person who is prone to OVERSTRESS, you must learn to look for its earliest warning signs. As soon as your sleep patterns change or you experience fatigue, lack of enjoyment of life, anxiety, or multiple aches and pains - that is the time to go through the OVERSTRESS checklist.

Rule -2: Exchange or postpone your stress.

Keep your stress level below your individual OVERSTRESS point by "exchanging stresses". If a new stress comes into your life, then make a room for it by eliminating or postponing another stress. This way, your TOTAL stress level remains low. The natural tendency is for people to let their stresses pile up rather than exchange them. In this fashion, OVERSTRESS gradually occurs. With the development of OVERSTRESS, the person starts using more and more Pick-Me-Ups, taking off on the wild roller coaster of ill health. IN ORDER TO STAY HEALTHY, LEARN TO EXCHANGE YOUR STRESSES.

Rule -3: Use these questions whenever you feel overstressed.

You now have a "*Questions Box*" full of ways to deal with your overstress. Whenever your body shows signs of overstress, you can use the tools from this book to help and set yourself back on the path of well-being. If you are feeling ill from stress, remember that troubled sleep, fatigue, aches, lack of enjoyment of life, and panic attacks are caused by chemical changes in your brain. Effective treatment can only be achieved if you act wisely, so if you feel overstressed and overwhelmed, try these questions and find the ways to relieve yourself.

Problem No 34 - How To Make Balance Between Home And Office

Stress Builder - My Home And My Office Life Is Not Adjusted. It Creates A Lot Of Stress To Me. What Should I Do?

Explanations- This is the most common problem in the big cities where the Father and the Mother are both working, and in spite of their separate Identities and earnings, Stress levels among the Women are increasing due to the imbalance in house and Office. It is really ironic that if a woman and her husband both work together and come home together, in spite of all odds, the woman always makes tea and refreshments for his husband. Although the time is changing, the real aspect remains the same. Women are always to be sought after all the household works in spite of all her busy schedules; either she is working as Doctor, C.A. or any other high-profile profession.

Gender Differences Related to Stress

This study is taken from the findings of a study done at the University of Alberta in Edmonton in 1989, with men and women who were parents of young children, with both parents working. In this study, they found that both men and women woke in the morning with relatively low levels of "stress", inducing hormones, although female levels were slightly higher than male.

However, a woman's stress enlarged throughout the time she was getting ready for work until she got to work, where it appealed much leveled out for the day. However, it increased significantly once she returned home at the end of the day.

Males, on the other hand, remained comparatively unstressed until they reached work, where stress levels increased throughout the day. There was some stress connected with traveling to and from work, but work created greater stress, and that stress dropped considerably upon a man's arriving at home. This may be explained by gender differences, where men find superior stress at work, and women find organization and the time at home more stressful.

The positive attitude for handling these different areas-

It is getting tougher these days to think of the glass as half full rather than half empty, but if you are going to survive this economic crisis- literally - you might try. That is a lesson from a large study of the death rates in optimistic Vs pessimistic women conducted by the researchers at the University of Pittsburgh. Using the data of women's health initiative, a study of more than 100,000 women over the age of 50 that began in 1994, the team found that optimistic women were 14% more likely to be alive than the pessimist peers.

At first, it is not surprising that optimistic people, being more hopeful overall, eat better, work out more and make regular visits to the doctor.

Another study shows that when it comes to the equality, men may be lagging behind in certain matters. ***For Instance***- The latest study by the McGill University Health Center shows that women have a more powerful immune system than men, which leads to better stress handling and disease fighting. The presence of estrogen has beneficial effects on innate immunity, which represents the body's first line of defense against pathogenic organisms. The results demonstrate that women have a more powerful inflammatory response than men.

Stress at work puts the same strain on the heart as being more than 18kg over weight; a study has relieved, and the prolonged bouts of tension have the same effects on the blood pressure as ageing 30 years. Therefore, the balance between the home and the office should be carefully maintained, which leads to the longer and healthier life.

Strategies for Stress Management and Better Balance Between Home and Office

Stress management is your ability to successfully manage the demands you feel at work and at home. When it comes to balancing between home and office, you don't have to go it alone. One of the advantages of working for a company and being part of a family system is that you have other people to provide you with support. By employing six strategies for stress management, you will begin to understand the assets you have around you.

Teamwork

The first stress management strategy is teamwork. When you are trying to achieve balance in your personal life and career, it's important to know when and what type of work you need to delegate and when you need to handle a responsibility on your own. At work, you let employees take on tasks that fit their skills and interests, in which areas of their jobs. If they are capable of certain tasks, this frees you up to do other important things.

Live in the Moment

Another strategy for stress management is to live in the moment. People who stay on the past or worry about the future have high levels of stress in their lives. Living in the moment on the job-relates to stress management because you react to challenges as they come up.

At home, living in the moment as a stress management tool is about smelling the roses and spending time with loved ones while they are alive.

Respect others

Putting yourself second is not the same thing as putting yourself last. Putting yourself second is a stress management philosophy that realizes the world does not rotate around you, and your ego does not hurt the emotional ground of other people around you. Treat yourself with the same amount of respect you would give others. When it comes to your clients as well as your family, you will only be able to offer them the best service and support when you are at your personal best. Your ideal stress management coping strategy is not about putting yourself first at the expense of your family and clients.

Be Cleverly Organized

Make space for daily, monthly and yearly goals, calendars and personal files for everyone with whom you have regular contact. Much of the stress we feel is because we have wasted so much time trying to find information on people or places we have lost and also declutter your life with many unimportant works. At home, we become frustrated when we lose our car keys or any of the things that were supposed to be at the right place.

Visualize

Try to visualize your success and the possible ways to achieve it. If you practice and calculate your resources to achieve your goal, you will better utilize your resources and possible help, which we often overlook in our daily lives.

Simplify your life

Know your limitations and qualities to deal with the problems. Simplify your life at home and at work. Do not expect too much and too unpractical targets for your self, which eventually create depression in later life.

Communicate with yourself

In order to maintain a good and stress-free life, communicate with yourself regularly. Try to find out - What is vital to meeting my goals? What goals do I have that might conflict with my purpose in life and my family? Am I expecting too much from others for my goals? These and several other types of questions can give you regular answers to your ambitions and your progress in life.

Problem No 35 - Behavior Related Stress By Your Boss

Stress Builder- My Boss Is Not Talking To Me Properly From Some Days. I Am Deeply Stressed And Feel Unsecured Due To This. What Should I Do?

Explanations- It is the most common thing most of the office workers deal with their daily affairs. If your boss is not dealing with you properly, there may be some reason behind it, but rather than looking at the real fact, you generally feels that there may be something fishy that lies in the attitude, and you are going to suffer from his behavior-related problem. This is not true at all. In practical, we all are living in this world with having a lot of problems lie ahead of us.

The expected cause for this problem-

- Your boss is, after all, a common man. He has a senior position in the office, but he is doing the same work and has the same family status as you have. When you have to share the same problems in your family matters, how can you forget that he also has a part to play. It may be possible that he has some personal problems in his family, and he is trying hard to find a solution for that. How can you expect him to behave with you normally when he/she is under the influence of great stress?

- There may be some health problem with him/her or any serious health-related problem recently diagnosed. In such events, any person can be stressed.

- In the office, there is a multiple channel of reporting. You enjoy the supremacy over a few people in the office; therefore, your boss enjoys that same status over you, and your seniors who work over him have other duties and responsibilities to do. The higher the post, the more important the part to be played; therefore, it may be possible that he/she is under pressure from his seniors and he may be suffering from job-related stress.

- Your boss has been recently transferred from a new place or is about to be transferred to a new office. In both the conditions, there is a possibility that he/she may be suffering from the emotional and job-related stress.

- Someone in the office has falsely told him/her about something bad about you, and he/she has made a bad impression of you. This is a serious problem that should be cleared up as earliest.

Supportive plans to combat this stress-

All these aspects are quite common and can convey the stress factor to the staff working under the particular boss. As far as the employee is concerned, all you can do to make a positive bridge with your boss to deal with this problem such as-

- Try to communicate with your boss in different matters other than office affairs. It will distract his concentration from the stress factor, and you might offer your help to deal with the crises.

- If possible, offer your Boss a tea or Coffee break. He will certainly find himself relaxed in the current stress. Moreover, you will come to know the real problem he is facing.

- If the attitude is created by someone in your office by telling him about something bad about you, when you offer to assist him, you will come to know the misunderstanding he has in your mind about you.

- Check out your performance; you might have missed any urgent task that is desperately needed by the Boss.

- And last, do not stress yourself as if you believe that you are doing your work properly, there is no need to create panic for yourself.

Problem No 36 - Stress Due To The Colleges In The Office

Stress Builder- My Colleagues Always Tell Stories About Me. I Know It Is All False, But It Stressed Me Always. How Can I Deal With Him?

Explanations- This is the most common problem in any office, and in some extent, everyone has suffered from it. In comparison, this problem is more common in the offices where the ladies workers are higher in numbers. The main reason behind these problems lies in the gender difference attitude. It has been seen that women usually clear their stress-related pressure in their office by discussing their problems with their colleagues or friends and asking for the possible solutions from them.

By doing this, ladies generally feel relaxed, but if the person to whom you have shared your problems disclosed it to other people in the office, you would certainly find yourself embarrassed and shocked. You may find backstabbed and betrayed, but it is really hard to find a perfect solution at this stage. Sometimes, the conditions become so worse that people are left with no option but to change the jobs, which is not so easy at this time of suppression.

Therefore, it is always good never to indulge in such a matter, which can cause you a great stress in your job.

Supportive plans to combat this stress-

There is not a particular guideline to deal with a problem, but there are certainly some points, which should be considered in an office atmosphere.

- There is an old English saying -

People who pat your back after your success are just looking for the right place to stab you in the future,

No matter how close your friendship is, but never ask for guidance in your very personal matter. Who knows, in future, he may not disclose your secret to other people or try to take advantage of your secret?

- The person you find capable of discussing your personal problems, may be known as a stupid or highly incapable person in the office. By getting the advice from that sort of person, you are most likely to add further vows to your current matter. By the time you realize the fact, it is too late to do anything.

- If you wish to chat with other colleagues in the office, stick to the limited topics and never cross the line into your personal matters. By doing this, you will never find yourself in trouble in the office.

- If you came to know that there have been rumors about you in the office, rather than stressing yourself or taking the leave, try to find the main culprit behind this, and face the situation boldly without getting emotional. The more you show your boldness, the sooner you will get out of these problems.

- Never show your extra sympathy or affection for any of your colleagues in the public. It may lead to some sort of misunderstanding about yourself.

Old Age Related Stress And Relationships Problems

Problem No 37 - Old Age Related Health Problems Which Can Increase Stress

Stress Builder - How Can I Make Myself Fit For Old Age And Stress?

Explanations- This is most common problem for the old age person in coping with his decreasing physical energy and with the increasing demands of his/her social and family responsibilities. These will not only give the great stress, but also its effects can give serious health problems. As you get older, your body's energy drops and the demands for nutrients increase. While the ageing is inevitable, many of the degenerative changes that prevail past middle age can be easily prevented. Recent medical studies and researches confirm that good nutrition can prevent or slow down the conditions such as osteoporosis, diabetes and heart disease. Along with the prevantations, the good diet can also boost up the mental level and energy to face the demands of growing responsibilities. Proper nutritious is the important part of any ageing strategy.

Changing Needs- A person's body composition changes with age. Muscle mass decreases due to increase in the fatty tissue. The metabolism slows down, and fewer calories are required. A 50 years old who needs 1800 calories a day will require 1440 calories at the age of 70 years. People who fail to cut the food in this age are likely to gain weight. With increasing age, the body is less efficient in absorbing some nutrients. An older person will need extra amounts of the following essential nutrients such as-

- Calcium to prevent osteoporosis and maintain healthy bone thinning problems. If you include the sesame and mustard seeds, leafy green, figs, mild and milk products in your diet, it can provide extra benefits.

- Vitamin D is needed in order to absorb the calcium in the body. The most economical source of the Vitamin D is the direct sunlight. If, for the 15 minutes, one stands in the open area in the morning between 10-11 A.M., the daily dose of required Vitamin D can be absorbed, free of cost.

- Vitamin B12 is very much essential for building red blood cells and maintaining healthy nerves.

- Zinc is required for the boost of lower immunity. Cereals, Nuts and Oil seeds are important sources of the Zinc.

- Folic Acids used to make the DNA and the red blood cells will help lower the risk of heart disease. By adding the Pulses and the legumes, such as Bengal Grams, along with the leafy vegetables can help a lot in overcoming these problems.

- Fiber is the most important thing to prevent constipation. Include Vegetables, fresh fruits and whole grains for these problems.
- One of the most important things is the water, which prevents the dehydration. Drink at least 10-12 glasses of water every day.

Emotional and Mental fitness for this age-

Although the nutrients play an important part in this phase of life, the healthy way of eating also plays an important part in this age to relieve the effects of emotional Stress.

- If you dislike eating alone, organize the regular potluck meals with friends and the family members.
- Select foods which are in good colors, texture and flavors. Avoid using extra salt to improve the flavors as it can be harmful; instead, use the spices and herbs.
- It helps to gather a good mix of ages around you - it will make the transition to old age more enjoyable.
- Try to go on a short vacation with a group of the same old people to a nearby religious spot or a hill station. It will not only give you enough pleasure but also give some freedom and relaxation for your family members also.
- Try not to interfere in the daily affairs of your family members; it will not only irritate them but it will also affect the personal relations.
- Try to develop a hobby. It is the best time to develop a long-forgotten hobby; you always wish to perform it.
- I have given a Stress Management programme in a Public Sector Company some time ago. It was specially meant for the senior citizens who are about to retire in the upcoming year. I was surprised to know that most of the people are quite stressed about how to spend their time after retirement. What they most fear is that they have to perform daily household work for their family, whether they like it or not. It is the most common thing in the present world. Once a person is retired from his regular job, he is supposed to do all the household jobs as he is a freely available to every single person for every single work required in the house, like - depositing all the Bills, buying the vegetables, milk, etc., repairing of all the items, etc. The problems are genuine and justified as to their views. I recommended a simple and the practical remedy to overcome these problems. I suggested that before they would be handed over the list of the household work from their sons, make a list of all the hobbies or the planning for only yourself and your wife to them. Your attitude towards yourself will change forever, and you will become free to do what you always wanted to do without any compulsion.
- Try to develop some of the activities like gardening and writing articles. It will not only help in physical strength but also prevent you from the age-related problem of Dementia.

- Maintain old friendships and make new contacts. Go for the walks in the park regularly.
- Exercise regularly in the form of walking or yoga to preserve the muscle strength, improve appetite and mood.
- If you have trouble in chewing, opt to have a vegetable puree or soup.
- Do not change your diet drastically; gradually include the nutrients and the requirements for the old age.

Child Stress Related Problems

Problem No 38 - When Your Child Is Depressed

Stress builder - My Child seems to be Depressed these days. What should I do to help him?

<u>**Explanations-**</u> Children have none of the stresses that we adults have, but the truth is, childhood is far from being without pressure in these days of changing lifestyles. Nuclear families, Loneliness, Academic pressure, etc. all are taking tolls on the young minds, which makes the childhood depressions on the rise.

We often hear our children complaining about stomach aches and nightmares, and it seems that learning about stress reduction is needed. This happens because even if there are no symptoms that the little one has a physical disorder, you know that something is wrong. If your pediatrician confirms that there is no disease disturbing your child, there is a great possibility that he simply suffers from stress.

What can you, as a parent, teacher or other concerned, help? The most important thing is to realize that children can become depressed just like adults, and you should help in the same manner as you deal with the adults. In fact, according to some international studies, one in the eight children is believed to have some sort of depression in his mind. In what concerns the causes of children's stress, usually, there are a few particular events in their lives that can produce serious damage to their fragile balance: their parents' divorce, the death of a loved person, moving to another city, frequent disputes in the family or intensive scholar activities.

In addition, tiredness caused by physical and psychological overload, nutrition deficiencies and lack of physical exercise normally leads to a stress condition. Therefore, learning about stress reduction and children is an essential lesson for any parent or individuals working with children for a better comprehension of their own problems and for helping them live a stress-free life.

Since childhood and adolescence are marked by the rapid changes in their bodies as well as their mind, many parents assume that the attitude, thoughts and feelings of their children are just stages that will be adjusted in the later life. In the process, they often make a mistake to read the vital signs of depression and stressed mind of their children.

Sources of Stress

Stress often comes from outside sources (such as family, friends, or school), but it can also come from within. The pressure we place on ourselves can be most important because there is often a difference between what we think we ought to be doing and what we are actually doing in our lives. Stress can concern anyone who feels weighed down, even kids. In preschoolers, separation from parents can cause anxiety. As kids get older, academic and social pressures create stress.

- *Too Busy for themselves*- Many kids are too busy to have time to play productively or relax after school. Kids who complain about the number of activities they're involved in or refuse to go to them may be signaling that they're overscheduled. Talk with your kids about how they feel about supplementary activities. If they complain, discuss about quitting one activity. If quitting isn't an option, explore ways to help manage your child's time and responsibilities so that they don't create so much anxiety.

- *Family atmosphere plays an important role*- Do your kids pay attention to you talking about troubles at work, worrying about a relative's illness, or fighting with your spouse about financial matters? Parents should watch how they talk about such issues when their kids are near because children will pick up on their parents' anxieties and start to worry themselves.

- *Receiving too much Knowledge about the world*- Believe it or not, the news can cause stress. Kids who see disturbing images on TV or hear talk about natural disasters, war, and terrorism may worry about their own safety and that of the people they love. Talk to your kids about what they see and hear, and monitor what they watch on TV so that you can help them understand what's going on.

- *Heartbreak in the family plays an important role-* Be aware of Stress-giving factors, such as an illness, the death of a loved one, or a divorce. When these are added to the everyday pressures kids face, the stress is magnified. Even the most agreeable divorce can be a difficult experience for kids because their basic protection system and their families are undergoing a tough change. Separated or divorced parents should never put kids in a position of having to choose sides or expose them to negative comments about the other spouse.

Signs that your child is depressed-

- Persistent Sadness.
- Hopelessness, irritability and gets easily agitated.
- Withdrawing from friends, family and even things they used to enjoy doing, such as participating in sports or doing a hobby like painting, reading, etc.
- Missing or skipping the school or decrease in school performances.
- Indecisive, forgetful and distracted.
- Feel guilty over the ways he or she feels.
- Having low esteem.
- Having regular health problems.

Supportive plans to combat this stress-

- If you see these signs and you perceive that your child is depressed, try to speak to the school child counselor or a proper psychotherapist for proper counselling and medications.

- As parents, we need to be sensitive to the child's emotions and insecurities. We must talk to them with full sincerity and look into their eyes as we do so. Most of the cases of child depression arise when there is not a favorable communication between the parents and the child, due to the busy schedule of the parents. I remember the case of a family where a son couldn't recognize his father after meeting him after a long time because his father was so busy in his shop that he usually came late at the night when the child was asleep, and the child left for the school when the father was sleeping in the morning. It is, in fact, a shocking incident, but it is generally happening in big cities.

- Keep vigil on the behavior of your child and ensure the lines of communication are open with your child.

- If possible take your family on a short vacation. Sometimes, the atmosphere of the house creates the stress to the child's behavior and depresses him.

- Children who are suffering from the major depression are more likely to suffer from the repeated bouts of depression; therefore, with a proper medications and monitoring, a child can be lifted back from the dark.

Following are some key rules while dealing about stress reduction, and children can help you guide your child in order to live a normal life. Here are the basic elements:

- Moral support- Let him feel you are always for your support.

- The ability to expect the stressful events or moments in your children's lives.

- Finding the best solution to remove the cause of stress and help your child live a gratifying and happy life.

- Guiding the child with weakness and attention when confronted with new situation in his life will always help him adapt better, be less puzzled and afraid, and thus prevent stressful situations.

- Your child needs things organized in his life. Make sure he knows that there are a few rules he has to follow and that he respects them: the eating hours, the bedtime hour or the time for play and time for study. This way, he will know what to do and when to do it. Never compare your children with other kids in family or in Society, etc. Every kid is unique, may he not good in studies but may be best in other fields; by comparing, you are just hurting your ego and self-respect.

- Prepare him for any changes in his life that might occur. He will adapt more easily to the new situations and learn how to be stretchy when changes occur.

- Never make a promise that you cannot respect. If you tell him you will give him a reward or that he will be grounded for something, don't try to find any reasons for delay because the child will lose its trust in you.

- Remember that in some moments, even if we want it or not, we can also contribute through our behavior at our children's stress. And even if we realize that we are making a mistake, most of the times, we just forget to correct ourselves.

Problem No 39 - Exam Related Stress Problems

Stress Builder- My Child Gets Highly Stressed In His Examination Days. What Should I Do To Relieve His Stress?

Explanations - Negativity and stress symptoms are on the rise in children around the world, which pose a high threat to their future, and the main reason for this behavior is their - **teachers and parents.** A survey has been conducted which gives the result that - the narrow mindset of the teachers and the parents are responsible for the emotional trauma students face these days. The survey, which was conducted by the **National Council for** Educational Research and Training (**NCERT**), 1100 school children were examined about their experiences in the class rooms. The survey reveals that there is an extreme trend of negativity among school children, which could impact their future lives.

The results show the particular results-

- Those children who are regularly scolded in the school develop poor learning abilities, whereever the soft-spoken teachers help in improving learning abilities.

- Beating, Scolding, Use of foul language, making children to read old chapters again and again and making them answer uneasy questions, which makes the negative effects on the Children.

- Teachers addressing the children with the words like - you are useless, can't do anything in life or good for nothing- in class rooms lower the children's self esteem and interest in learning.

- Poor class room atmosphere impacts a student's learning abilities.

I have conducted a stress management survey in a large school. Before conducting the survey I was not so sure about the result, but when the result came out, it really shocked me. Most of the students have been facing the top most stress in their lives. The common view they share was that they were totally disoriented in their lives. Their teachers demanded particular things, their father expected a certain things and mother expected something extra. They were totally confused as no body cared about their own choice, and moreover, they were so busy with studies that they could hardly get any time to nourish their own hobbies or likings.

The study also revealed that they felt extremely happy and less stressed when they were taught something new or in an innovative manner.

Students who suffer from test anxiety tend to worry about achievement in school, especially when doing well on tests. They worry about the future and are awfully self-critical. Instead of feeling challenged by the prospect of success, they become afraid of collapse. This makes them anxious about tests and their own abilities. Ultimately, they become so worked up that they feel incompetent about the subject matter or the test.

Suggestions for Overcome Exam Stress

It does not help to tell the child to relax without knowing the real methods or stop worrying. But there are ways to reduce test nervousness. Support your child to do these things:

- Keep yourself busy; look at the rational assumptions of problems and also the alternative solutions.

- Do not fuss about the little things. Do not let little things ruin your happiness.

- Avoid being standing in the company of the class mates or friends who always find the negative in the positive side of life.

- Space studying over days or weeks. Be aware of the information and relate it to what is already known. Review it more than once. (By doing this, the student should feel prepared at exam time.)

- Be aware of all the feelings experienced due to the stress.

- Bury the past, which is dead.

- Physical exercises like - Deep Breathing and Meditation can ease the problems.

- Be in the sync with the natural sleep-wake cycle.

- Don't "cram" the night before-cramming increases anxiety, which interferes with clear thinking. Get a good night's sleep. Rest, exercise, and eating well are as important to test-taking as they are to other schoolwork.

- Read the directions carefully when the teacher hands out the test. If you don't understand them, ask the teacher to explain

- Look quickly at the entire examination to see what types of questions are included (multiple choice, matching, true/ false, essay) and, if possible, the number of points for each. This will help you pace yourself

- If you don't know the answer to a question, skip it and go on. Don't waste time worrying about it. Mark it so you can identify it as unanswered. If you have time at the end of the exam, return to the unanswered questions.

- Write down the positive affirmation statements before sleep. This will certainly enhance self-confidence and increase family bonds. for Example-

1. I am free from Worry – Tension - Stress – Anxiety - Anger - Pain
2. I have good memory - focus - attention.
3. I have good confidence in myself.
4. I have good relations with my family, and they will help me in all circumstances.

- When an option is not visible, sleep over the problem; you might find the answer next morning. The brain works calmly when you sleep.
- While there is nothing like making and following a time table, ever so often, it happens that the timetable, no matter how perfect on paper, goes haywire after the first few days, and the students find him in a fizzy at the last minutes. A good way to deal with these types of problems is to prepare and revise them regularly for the days before the exams will be highly beneficial.

A recent study-related guideline I would like to add for the benefit of exam stress-

M.U.R.D.E.R. the exams- **Adapted from John R.Hayes -**

- <u>Mood-</u> Set a positive mood for yourself to study in and select the appropriate time and attitude.
- <u>Understanding-</u> Mark any information you do not understand in a particular unit and keep focus on one unit at a time.
- <u>Recall</u>- After studying the unit, stop and put what you have learned in your own words.
- <u>Expect realistically-</u> Nobody knows you as well as you do yourself, so be realistic in your expectations from yourself.
- <u>Review-</u> Go over the material you have covered. Review what strategies helped you understand and retain information in the past.

Guidelines for Parents- There are some guidelines for the parents also to help in maintaining positive attitudes towards their children-

- Show Support to your child rather than compare him with other children in the school, Block or in relations.
- Remember that your child is unique and different from other children. Accept his shortcomings and try to improve his hidden qualities.
- Do not expect too unrealistic targets from your children; it will put additional stress on their little minds.
- Take care of his diet required for his tough and demanding days.
- Never discuss his study plans with any one; it will not only misguide you but also put additional pressure on your child's study plan, which results in a disaster.
- Keep the home atmosphere calm and supportive as much as you can; a little disturbance can stress your child's mind.

Problem No 40 - Child Obesity And Eating Habits

Stress Builder- My Child Eats Whatever And Whenever He Likes. His Obesity And Health Give Me A Lot Of Stress. What Should I Do?

<u>Explanations-</u> In the U.S., at least one out of five kids is overweight. The number of overweight children continues to grow in rapid figures. Over the last two decades, this number has increased by more than 50%, and the number of "exceptionally" overweight children has nearly doubled.

A doctor determines if children are overweight by measuring their height and weight. Although children have fewer weight-related health problems than adults, overweight children are at high risk of becoming overweight adolescents and adults. Overweight adults are at risk for a number of health problems, including heart disease, diabetes, high blood pressure, stroke, and some forms of cancer.

Some Facts about child obesity-

- Obese children and adolescents have shown an alarming increase in the occurrence of type 2 diabetes due to the poor habits of eating junk foods and sedentary lifestyle.
- Many obese children have high cholesterol and blood pressure levels, which are risk factors for heart disease.
- One of the most severe problems for obese children is sleep apnea (interrupted breathing while sleeping) and less regular sleep according to their age. In some cases, this can lead to problems with learning and memory.
- Obese children have a high incidence of orthopedic problems, liver disease, asthma and several other deadly diseases in their lives.
- Children become overweight for a variety of reasons. The most common causes are genetic factors, lack of physical activity, unhealthy eating patterns, eating under the influence of stress, or a combination of these factors. There may be an endocrine disorder that may cause a child to become overweight.
- Genetic Factors: Children whose parents or brothers or sisters are overweight may be at an additional increased risk of becoming overweight themselves. Genetic factors play a significant role in increasing overweight problems, but shared family behaviors such as eating and activity habits also influence body weight.
- Lifestyle: A child's total diet and his or her activity level both play an important role in deciding a child's weight. The increasing popularity of television and computer and video games contributes to children's inactive lifestyles. Apart from this, the use of

junk foods along with the use of Colas, while watching the T.V. is also a major part of this Problem.

- A recent Swedish study reveals that the risk of obesity in the teenage children is comparably equal to smoking up to 10 cigarettes per day. The study suggests that the normal weight, heavy smokers and the non-smokers obese have the same risk factors.

Supportive plans to combat this stress-

There is a major part to get away from this problem is to adopt a helpful and supportive attitude towards your child rather than adopting the negative and penalizing him for a fault, for which you may be equally responsible in some way.

- Be Supportive of your child's problems- One of the most important things you can do to help overweight children is to let them know that they are okay whatever their weight is, which does not make them feel shameful and neglected about themselves. If you accept your children at any weight and appearance, they will be more likely to accept and feel good about themselves. It is also important to talk to your children about weight, as it allows them to share their concerns with you. Your child probably knows better than anyone else that he or she has a weight problem. For this reason, overweight children need support, acceptance, and encouragement from their parents.

- Try to combine the issue as a family matter- Parents should not make the children away from each other because of their weight and appearance, but should spotlight on regularly changing their family's physical activity and eating habits. Family involvement helps to teach everyone healthy habits and does not single out overweight children.

- Minimize your family's sedentary lifestyle- Indulge the family in habitual physical activity, combined with healthy eating habits with low-fat diets, is the most efficient and healthful way to control your weight. It is also an important part of a healthy and disease free lifestyle. Some simple ways to increase your family's physical activity include the following:

  1. Rather than spending more time indoor, try to spend more free time in the recreation center or a park with your children. Because your children will accept you as a Role model. If your children see that you are physically active and have fun, they are more likely to be active and stay active for the rest of their lives.

  2. Plan family activities that provide everyone with exercise and enjoyment, like walking, dancing, biking, or swimming. For example, schedule a walk with your family after dinner instead of watching TV. This type of exercise not only provides health but also makes healthy communication network between the family members.

- ***Be sensitive to your child's needs-*** Overweight children may feel painful about participating in certain activities. It is important to help your child find physical activities that they enjoy, which aren't uncomfortable or too difficult.

- ***Do indulge in a sedentary lifestyle-*** Reduce the amount of time you and your family spend in sedentary activities, such as watching TV, playing video games or doing computers without any justified reasons. This will not only save your child from excess eye strain but also help in maintaining weight.

- **_Be an ideal for your Family_**- Become more active throughout your day and encourage your family to do so as well. For example, walk up the stairs instead of taking the elevator or carry out certain activities during a work or school half break, like stretching exercises or walking around.

- **_Try to adopt healthy eating habits-_** Adopting healthy eating practices early will help children approach eating with the right attitude that food should be enjoyed and is necessary for growth, development, and for energy to keep the body running. Find out more about children's nutritional needs by reading or talking with a health professional, and allow your children to choose what and how much they eat.

- **_Do not force your children for a particular diet_**- Children should never be placed on a restrictive diet to lose weight unless a doctor supervises one for justified medical reasons. Limiting what children eat may be harmful to their health and interfere with their growth and development.

- **_Restrict the fat intake_**- Reducing fat is a good way to cut calories without affecting your child's nutrients. Simple ways to cut the fat in your family's diet include eating low-fat or non-fatty dairy products. However, major efforts to change your child's diet should be under medical supervision.

- **_Introduce healthy eating options at home-_** Introduce the extensive variety of healthful foods available in the house. This practice will help your children learn how to make healthy food choices rather than going for junk food available in the market.

- **_Try safe eating habits_**- Develop and teach healthy eating habits, like eating at a slow pace, which will make your child detect hunger and fullness better when eating slowly.

- **_Encourage eating together_**- Studies show that eating together can develop strong family bonds, so try to make mealtimes pleasant with conversation and sharing, not a time for scolding or arguing.

- **_Discourage your child to eat in front of watching T.V._**-Try to eat only in chosen areas of your home, such as the dining room or kitchen. Eating in front of the T.V. may make it difficult to pay attention to thoughts of fullness and may lead to overeating.

- **_Do not use food as a tool-_** Using food as a tool is a highly unjustified way to deal with your child. Forbidding him to take certain food punishment may lead children to worry that they will not get enough food. when foods, such as sweets, are used as a reward, children may assume that these foods are more valuable than other foods

- **_Keep an eye on the food outside the home-_** Try to find out more about your school lunch program, or pack your child's lunch to include a variety of foods. Also, select healthier items, which will discourage him from taking outside foods.

Problem No 41 - Teen Behavior Related Problems

Stress Builder- My Teenage Child is highly disruptive behavior and rude. This gives me lots of stress at home. What should I do?

Explanations- There may be one justified reason behind this problem, which can be a Burning out phase of stress. Believe it or not, this is quite possible in today's fast-paced life. School, sports, extra curricular activities, high demands in studies, friends, boyfriend/girlfriend relationships and family demand time and attention from your teen. So much so that he could be experiencing signs of stress, or worse - burnout. There are several signs of the burnout that you should be on the lookout for his indecent behavior-

- Your teenager is acting depressed. He doesn't want to do anything, he has lost interest in things he likes to do, and he has reduced concentration when doing things.

- Your teenager is feeling some anxiety for no known reason, or he is acting over-anxious and restless. He hardly relaxes, is not sleeping well, is unable to get to sleep at night or has disturbed sleep patterns.

- Your teenager is either overeating or under eating, as both are a response to being stressed.

- Your teenager is giving in rude behavior, more than normal, and is showing signs of emotional instability.

- Your teenager is experiencing neck or back pain along with Headaches.

- Your teenage daughter is missing or having irregular menstrual cycles.

- Your teenager is complaining of upset stomach, dizziness, dryness of throat and mouth and drinks excess or too little water in a day.

- Your teenager has emotional tension and alertness, and a penetrating voice or easily gets irritated by minor issues.

- Increased risk-taking or over careless about daily affairs can be a sign of burnout.

Along with these, there may be some more signs of the problems, such as

Emotional Disturbances such as
1. Disbelief
2. Anxiety

3. Fearfulness
4. Stick to Parents
5. Guilt
6. Inner conflicts
7. Hopelessness and Helplessness attitude.

Physical signs-
1. Regressive Behavior (ex., thumb-sucking bedwetting)

Social / Behavioral-
1. Disappearance of valuable items or money.
2. Not coming home on time.
3. Not telling you where they are going.
4. Constant excuses for behavior.
5. Spending a lot of time in their rooms.

Lies about activities-
1. finding the following: cigarette rolling papers, pipes, roach clips, small glass vials, plastic baggies, leftovers of drugs

Signs at School-
1. Sudden drop in grades
2. Poor interest in learning
3. Sleeping in class
4. Poor work performance
5. Not doing homework
6. Defiant of authority
7. Poor attitude toward sports or other extracurricular activities
8. Not informing you of teacher meetings, open houses, etc.

Changes in friends and Lifestyle-
1. Smell of alcohol on breath or body
2. Doesn't seem as happy as they used to be
3. Overly tired or energetic
4. Drastic weight loss or gain

As compared to the Adult person stress scale, Teenage children have to face different levels of stress and their effects, which are described below-

Stress Scale For The Teen Age Youth-

STRESS	EVENT VALUE
DEATH OF SPOUSE, PARENT, BOYFRIEND/GIRLFRIEND	100
DIVORCE of your parents	65
PUBERTY	65
PREGNANCY (or causing pregnancy)	65
MARITAL SEPARATION OR BREAKUP WITH BOYFRIEND/GIRLFRIEND	60
JAIL TERM OR PROBATION	60
DEATH OF OTHER FAMILY MEMBER (other than spouse, parent or boyfriend/girlfriend)	60
BROKEN ENGAGEMENT	55
ENGAGEMENT	50
SERIOUS PERSONAL INJURY OR ILLNESS	45
MARRIAGE	45
ENTERING COLLEGE OR BEGINNING THE NEXT LEVEL OF SCHOOL	45
CHANGE IN INDEPENDENCE OR RESPONSIBILITY	45
ANY DRUG AND/OR ALCOHOL USE	45
FIRED AT WORK OR EXPELLED FROM SCHOOL	45
CHANGE IN ALCOHOL OR DRUG USE	45
RECONCILIATION WITH MATE, FAMILY OR BOYFRIEND/GIRLFRIEND (getting back together)	40
TROUBLE AT SCHOOL	40

SERIOUS HEALTH PROBLEM OF A FAMILY MEMBER	40
WORKING WHILE ATTENDING SCHOOL	35
WORKING MORE THAN 40 HOURS PER WEEK	35
CHANGING COURSE OF STUDY	35
CHANGE IN FREQUENCY OF DATING	35
SEXUAL ADJUSTMENT PROBLEMS	35
GAIN OF NEW FAMILY MEMBER (new baby born or parent remarries or adopts)	35
CHANGE IN WORK RESPONSIBILITIES	35
CHANGE IN FINANCIAL STATE	30
DEATH OF A CLOSE FRIEND (not a family member)	30
CHANGE TO A DIFFERENT KIND OF WORK	30
CHANGE IN NUMBER OF ARGUMENTS WITH MATE, FAMILY OR FRIENDS	30
SLEEP LESS THAN 8 HOURS PER NIGHT	25
TROUBLE WITH IN-LAWS OR BOY/GIRLFRIEND'S FAMILY	25
OUTSTANDING PERSONAL ACHIEVEMENT (awards, grades, etc.)	25
MATE OR PARENTS START OR STOP WORKING	20
BEGIN OR END SCHOOL	20
CHANGE IN LIVING CONDITIONS (visitors in the home, remodeling house, change in roommates)	20
CHANGE IN PERSONAL HABITS (start or stop a habit like smoking or dieting)	20

CHRONIC ALLERGIES	20
TROUBLE WITH THE BOSS	20
CHANGE IN WORK HOURS	15
CHANGE IN RESIDENCE	15
CHANGE TO A NEW SCHOOL (other than graduation)	10
PRESENTLY IN PRE-MENSTRUAL PERIOD	15
CHANGE IN RELIGIOUS ACTIVITY	15
GOING IN DEBT (you or your family)	10
CHANGE IN FREQUENCY OF FAMILY GATHERINGS	10
VACATION	10
PRESENTLY IN WINTER HOLIDAY SEASON	10
MINOR VIOLATION OF THE LAW	5

Remedies to deal with these Problems-

Learning how to deal with stress is a part of growing up, but your teen will need your help. Here are seven tips that will help you and help him:

- *Talk to your child*. If you're never there for your teen, you won't be able to help him. Take some time out of your week for some one-on-one time with him. Make this part of your routine so that your teenager will know that he can count on you being there.

- *Break his Daily same boring routine-* Teenager Children use the benefits of taking the dog out for a jog, hiking a trail, or just going out for a walk. Physical activity is known to relieve stress. Creativity will also help to relieve stress. Buy your teenager a diary or encourage another creative hobby.

- *Make him Laugh*- Laughter can get rid of stress just as much as exercise and is another healthy escape. Make comic or humorous books available in your home. Allow get-togethers with friends. Rent movies with a comedy theme. You can also teach your teen how to laugh at himself rather than at another person. Using humor to take the stress away from normal human mistakes that can happen.

- Build your teenager's confidence and self-esteem by praising him when he does something good. Make this a habit by finding something your teenager did right every day. It's not that they aren't doing good things all the time. The parents are the basic foundation of confidence and self-esteem that you provide, and then your teenager will be better able to handle changes and stress.

- Teach your teenager how to keep things in standpoint. This is an important part of relieving stress. Taking a situation and looking at it from different points of view and seeing how it relates to the whole scheme of life is a skill your teenager will need to learn from your experiences.

- Show your teenager how to focus on the positive aspects of a situation. Have him try and list the benefits and opportunities created rather than the problems. Even the most unpleasant experiences can lead to positive growth and outcomes.

- Be wary of negative roadblocks. Often, teenagers who do not learn how to deal with stress properly turn to drugs and alcohol. Talk to your teen often about these roadblocks and remember the warning signs.

- One important listening skill to use when communicating with your teenager is using Door Openers, as opposed to Door Slammers. Door Openers are open-ended responses that do not convey evaluation or judgment. Door Slammers are just the opposite. They convey to your teenager that you do not wish to have this discussion with them.

Examples of Door Openers or the welcome gestures to your child-

1. "What do you think?"
2. "Would you like to share more about that?"
3. "That's a good question."
4. "I don't know, but I'll find out"
5. "I'm interested in what you are saying."
6. "Do you know what that means?"
7. "That sounds important to you."
8. "Do you want to talk about it?"

Examples of Door Slammers or non-welcome gestures to your child–

1. "You are too young to understand."
2. "If you say that again, I'll..."
3. "That's none of your business."
4. "I don't care what your friends are doing!"
5. "We'll talk about that when you need to know."
6. "That's just for boys/girls"

7. "Why are you asking me that?"
8. "You don't need to know about that."

One of the lesser known Therapies for Stress reduction in TeenAge children is the Pet Therapy. Having a pet Dog can be highly beneficial for the behavior of your child such as the following effects-

Benefits of Pet Therapy-

- *Pets Encourage You To Get Out And Exercise:* Whether we walk our dogs because they need it or are more likely to enjoy a walk when we have companionship, dog owners do than non-pet owners, at least if we live in an urban setting. Because exercise is good for stress management and overall health, owning a dog can be credited with increasing these benefits.

- *Pets Can Help With Social Support:* When we're out walking, having a dog with us can make us more approachable and give people a reason to stop and talk, thereby increasing the number of people we meet, giving us an opportunity to increase our network of friends and acquaintances, which also has great stress management benefits.

- *Pets Stave Off Loneliness and Provide Unconditional Love*: Pets can be there for you in ways that people can't. They can offer love and companionship, and can also enjoy comfortable silence and keep secrets. And they could be the best antidote to loneliness. In fact, research shows that nursing home residents reported less loneliness when visited by dogs than when they spent time with other people! All these benefits can reduce the amount of stress people experience in response to feelings of social isolation and lack of social support from people.

- *Pets Can Reduce Stress- Sometimes, More Than People:* While we all know the power of talking about your problems with a good friend who's also a good listener, recent research shows that spending time with a pet maybe even better! Recent studies show that when conducting a task that's stressful, people actually experience less stress when their pets are with them than when a supportive friend or even their spouse is present! (This may be partially due to the fact that pets don't judge us; they just love us.)

- *Create a feeling of helping hand-* Teenage children often learn and feel from providing the daily food, bathing and combing hairbrush to their pets, the value of dependencies in general life, by which they will become good parents in the future.

Problem No 42 - Concentration On Studies

Stress Builder- My Child Finds It Very Hard To Concentrate In Studies. It Gives Him Lots Of Stress. How Can I Help Him?

Explanation- This is the most common problem of today's children. With having so much of entertaining and enjoyable methods like computer games, computers, fun parks, Mobile and many more, They find it really hard to concentrate their mind on studying various topics. This will not only bring extra stress into their lives but also create tension for their parents when the results appear. There are a number of tried and tested techniques for improving memory. These strategies have been established within cognitive psychology literature and suggest great ways to improve memory, to remember better and to appear well in the examinations-

Supportive plans to combat this stress-

- **Focus your consideration on the study materials**- Attention is one of the major components of memory. In order for information to move from short-term memory into long-term memory, you need to actively attend to this information. Try to study in a place free from distractions, such as television, music, and other diversions.

- **Get organized**- Researchers have found that information is organized in memory in related groups. You can take advantage of this by structuring and organizing the materials you are studying. Try grouping similar concepts and terms together, or make an outline of your notes and textbook readings to help group related concepts.

- **Utilize mnemonic devices to remember information-** Mnemonic devices are a technique often used by students to aid in recall. A mnemonic is simply a way to remember information. For example, you might associate a term you need to remember with a common item you are very familiar with. The best mnemonics are those that utilize positive imagery, humor, or novelty. You might come up with a rhyme, song, or joke to help remember a specific segment of information

For example, if we try to learn important in the form of a Song lyrics from a famous Movie, we will remember the whole thing in seconds.

Review the information you are studying- In order to recall information, you need to program what you are studying into long-term memory. One of the most effective encoding techniques is known as elaborative rehearsal. An example of this technique would be to read the definition of a key term, study the definition of that term, and then read a more detailed description of what that term means. After repeating this process a few times, your recall of the information will be far better.

- **Speak about new information-** When you are studying unfamiliar material, take the time to think about how this information relates to things that you already know. By establishing relationships between new ideas and previously existing memories, you can dramatically increase the likelihood of recalling the recently learned information.

- **Visualize concepts to improve memory and recall-** Many people benefit greatly from visualizing the information they study. Pay attention to photographs, charts, and other graphics in your textbooks. If you don't have visual cues to help, try creating your own. Draw charts or figures in the margins of your notes or use highlighters or pens in different colors to group related ideas in your written study materials.

- **Teach new concepts to another person-** Research suggests that reading materials out loud significantly improves memory of the material. Educators and psychologists have also discovered that having students actually teach new concepts to others enhances understanding and recall. You can use this approach in your own study by teaching new concepts and information to a friend or study partner.

- **Pay extra concentration to difficult information-** Have you ever noticed how it's sometimes easier to remember information at the beginning or end of a chapter? Researchers have found that the position of information can play a role in recall, which is known as the serial position effect. While recalling middle information can be difficult, you can overcome this problem by spending extra time rehearsing this information or trying to restructure the information, so it will be easier to remember.

- **Vary your study routine-** Another great way to increase your recall is occasionally changing your study routine. If you are accustomed to studying in one specific location, try moving to a different spot to study. If you study in the evening, try to spend a few minutes each morning reviewing the information you studied the previous night. By adding an element of novelty to your study sessions, you can increase the effectiveness of your efforts and significantly improve your long-term recall.

- **Self Negative Talk-** It generally happens when we feel the work is too difficult. We generally presume that we are unable to achieve the target and indulge in Negative self-talk, like we are hopeless, this work is too difficult for me to do, I am too incapable of doing this work, etc. This will not only harm our self image but also hamper our ability to achieve the target. Therefore never make any poor or negative comments to yourself.

Having a sharp memory in mind can be as simple as finding ways to help jog your memory throughout the day. Here are 10 quick ideas:

- **Put in writing it down-** With the number of things you have to remember on any given day, why should you try to stuff it all into your memory bank? When you want to remember something, the very best thing to do is write it down. Then, when you need to recall it, it will be there for you in an instant

- **Keep it jointly-** When you write down things you want to remember, keep them in one consistent place. Otherwise, you're going to spend a lot of time looking for your notes.

- **Maintain good health-** Eat healthy foods, get enough sleep, and do exercise. These are all important for your memory, staying focused and being alert

- **Record your thoughts-** Sometimes, you might want to remember something, but it's impossible for you to write it down, such as when you're driving. A little hand held voice recorder on your mobile phone is a wonderful gadget to carry around with you and record your thoughts, your parking space number, or a phone number you see on a billboard

- **Think positive-** If you keep saying you have a bad memory, you'll probably continue to have a bad memory. It's important to have motivation; I CAN remember attitude.

- **Post sticky note reminders-** Those colourful, little sticky notes can be amazing memory helpers. Want to remember something before you leave your place? Jot it down on a Post-It Note and stick it on the inside of your door. You'll be sure to see it as you're getting ready to walk out. Have to make an urgent call first thing in the morning? Leave a Post-It Note on your telephone

- **Set timers and alarms-** Take advantage of alarm clocks and timers throughout the day. Use visual reminders. Visual reminders can help you remember and focus. I especially like visual reminders for remembering your goals. If your goal is to take a trip to a beautiful island in a few years, keep a magazine photograph of the island right on your desk. If your goal is to own your own business one day, find a picture or ornament that will help remind you of this goal each day.

- **Give yourself time to form a memory** - Memories are quickly lost in the short-term, and disturbances can make you forget. When meeting a new person, are you listening and concentrating? The key to avoiding losing memories before they have even formed is to give yourself time to focus on things without allowing yourself to be distracted.

- **Repeat things** - A nice and easy one; this is a no-brainer, but the more times you hear, see, or think about something, the more you'll remember it! That new person you met, try repeating their name, writing it down, and thinking about it. You'll remember it.

- **Get your life organized** - Put your keys, wallet and phone in the same place every time you come home. Get a diary or organizer to keep track of your appointments, bills, birthdays and anniversaries. I know this won't improve your memory, but it will free your mind from the routine things in life and allow you to concentrate on memory improvement. Plus, in my case, it greatly reduced stress

- **An exceptional exercise**- I have heard about an exercise which can rapidly enhance the functioning of the mind. It is a very simple exercise like – trying to do the things which we generally do with a right or common hand. Try to do certain things daily with your opposite hand, like tooth brushing, shoe polishing, writing, etc. This process will activate the opposite side of your mind, and with regular exercise, you will achieve the power of strong memory.

Problem No 43 - Poor Time Management Leads To Stress

Stress Builder- I Always Gets Late In Paying For My Bills, It Costs Me Penalty And A Lots Of Stress

Explanations- This is the most common problem which we all share in some manner. We all live in the modern world, and we all buy all sorts of necessities and luxuries from different sources. All the purchases we make, and are divided into two types-

- *Direct purchases*- Like grocery from the local vendors or market who do not have any credit card facilities with him, therefore we have to pay them on a cash basis. It usually does not give much stress as we know how much we are supposed to pay as per the pocket allows.

- *Indirect purchase*- It consist of all the purchases for which the bill is generated after the desired amount of product is used. It includes the bill for electricity, water, credit cards, telephones and many other things. The bill of the usage of the facility is supposed to be deposited at the specific time; failing to do so, there is usually a heavy penalty along with the discontinuation of the usage of the services can be ruled out.

We all are so busy in our daily bread and butter affairs that we often tend to ignore or postpone the billing details, and when the last date arrives for the payments, we find ourselves under the great stress as the priority to deposit the bill is the utmost, and we often find our schedule very tight to deal with this problem. Efficient time management is one of the ways to manage stress in our lives. In the world of technology and computers, all designed to make our lives easier and add to our free time, day by day, we are ultimately busier than ever. Single or with family responsibilities, we must all find ways to organize and manage our time so that we get little time for our own personal pleasure and relaxation. Our time is our life. The more we are able to plan and manage our time in an effective manner, the more we will be able to enjoy our lives.

But, not everyone has the gift of efficient organization and proper time management. Often many people feel that they are demoralized by the many things they have to do for their families, home and work.

The pressures felt by the uncontrolled flow of things we have to do during working hours are increasing, and eventually, they become unbearable by the additional requirements that currently exist in our personal and family life.

Supportive plans to combat this stress-

- *Generate a to-do list-* Initially, we can make a list of our daily obligations, or even with the obligations we have to perform in the near future, specifying when and how our obligations will be met. Repetitive obligations can be planned for specific days and times when we have the appropriate time and availability to finish them. We must never forget that the planning and designing our activities for each day gives us a large degree of control over our time. We must recognize what is important for us and be placed first on our list.

- *Create 'smart' arrangements -* Plan the most difficult things you have to do at the beginning of the week so you are more relaxed by the weekend. For difficult tasks, it is better to place them on Monday or Tuesday, while most mechanical jobs are around the middle of the week, leaving Thursday and Friday free and more relaxed as these two days accumulate the fatigue and stress from the work of the rest of the week.

- *Find extra time for yourself-* If you wake up half an hour earlier in the morning, you will earn a little extra time for yourself. Also, you can achieve the same if you sleep half an hour later. Half an hour of sleep makes no difference in our rest of the day but can give us comfort in our daily activities.

- *Get your main concern right-* We must learn to put priorities. English says, "First things, first!" The most important tasks must be first and ranked first in our priorities. Do not neglect your important tasks to achieve the insignificant.

- *Delegation-* Try to share some of your obligations and tasks with other family members or with other colleagues in your work if you feel that you cannot anticipate everything. In this way, you manage to reduce stress and achieve effectiveness in dealing with anything. At the same time, what you choose to do, do it right and save time for yourself. The art of transferring work to others can provide many benefits to people with managerial positions who are usually overburdened by obligations.

- *Start from the right step-* We need to be careful when we are engaged with important and quality tasks. It is preferable from the beginning to do such jobs carefully and correctly because experience shows that we might need more time to do the necessary corrections afterwards.

- *Break long jobs into smaller tasks-* Another technique that can help us in managing both stress and our time is to break down long tasks that are usually unwanted or difficult into smaller tasks. We can, for example, every day, systematically to spend ten minutes on unwanted or difficult works. When you start this way, it is possible to understand that you are progressing and that the completion of such work will come quickly.

- *Don't try to be perfect-* You should limit the perfection, which dominates most of us. The pointless game of perfection in trivial things is a waste of time and restricts us from dealing with something else.

- ***Sort out to-do lists*-** Equally important is to recognize what is not so essential for us and remove it from our to-do lists. Here, we must be very harsh on our choices. Removal from our schedule tasks that are not crucial will free our time, which we can use for rest and for other things that are more important.

- ***Practice better Self-Control*-** We should always control ourselves in regards to the activities we perform. We need to thoroughly examine how we spend our time every day. If necessary, for a few days, we can write all our activities on a paper. Then, we will examine our activities and enhance our time. We must look for how we can remove or modify some activities for us to gain more time.

- ***Do not forget entertainment and rest-*** As effective and efficient as we can be, we must never forget that our time is short and precious and must be respected. It is good to avoid things that burden us psychologically and learn to be creative and happy in our everyday lives. We must not forget to entertain ourself, because a lack of entertainment in our lives leads to emotional fatigue, which is easily converted into physical tiredness. Save time for yourself; you ought to have it!

Problem No 44 - Vacation Related Stress

Stress Builder - Whenever I Go Out For Vacations, I Fear An Unknown Stress Several Days Before The Trip Begins. How Can I Stop This?

Explanations- This type of stress is faced by almost all of us to some extent. We all fear that the place we are visiting, rather than reducing our stress, may not increase our stress level, and all the unknown fears related to travel also hamper our minds. Before we talk about the effects of stress, we should look at the reasons why we should have vacations to reduce everyday stress.

- *Vacations support inspiration*: A good vacation can help us to reconnect with ourselves; working as a vehicle for self-discovery and helping us get back to feeling our best.

- *Vacations reduce the Burnout effects*: Office workers who take regular time to relax are less likely to experience burnout, making them more inspired and dynamic than their overworked counterparts.

- *Vacations can keep us in good physical shape*: Taking regular time off to 'recharge your batteries', thereby keeping stress levels lower, can keep you healthier and disease-free.

- *Vacations can make stronger family Bonds*: Spending time enjoying life with loved ones can keep relationships strong, helping you enjoy the good times more and helping you through the stress of the hard times. In fact, a study by the Arizona Department of Health and Human Services found that women who took vacations were more satisfied with their marriages

- *Unlimited places to explore-* There are endless places in the world where one can go and relax along with lots of shopping and eating options which can give immense pleasures known to mankind

Stress factors and vacations-

What we fear about -

- Getting good accommodating places to the destinations.
- Missing the flight /train in the middle of the way.
- Any mishappening, like - theft, accident, baggage loss, etc.
- Any unfortunate incident at home in the absence.

- Any serious health problems.
- Fear of the unknown?

All these fears are quite common and are quite justified in some way, but I have seen that the stress-related to these affairs dominates the mind and often spoils the mood and excitement of the family members as well.

Supportive plans to combat this stress-

- *Make proper study about destinations* - Before making a plan to any destination; try to get all the related information about the accommodations, transportation, and famous tourist destinations well in advance. You can search the Internet, Tourist information centers, and your friends or relatives who are well aware of that very place because the more you plan in advance, the less you are going to be stressed in the middle of journey. Nowadays lots of Apps provide packages for any destination in the world; if you feel you cannot manage, hire them at the best rates.

- *Prepare to get travel insurance* - Investing in travel insurance and also in health insurance can prevent you from any misfortune related after effects.

- *Plan in advance -* Basically, much of the stress incurred by traveling has to do with simple worries, like missing your plane or forgetting vital documents, such as passports or travellers' cheques. This is easy to conquer if you take positive action. Ensure you arrive at the airport well before you're required to check in, whether this means calling a taxi before you normally would or getting an earlier train. This way, you know for sure that there's no chance of you being late, even if trains get cancelled, or there's traffic on the motorway.

- *Prevent your House* - Prevent your house from any calamity by adopting simple methods like
    1. Safe guard your valueable assets in the safe custody of bank lockers.
    2. Install protective door alarms and siren or remote cameras.
    3. Inform the neighbors about the durations and expected day of arrival.
    4. Inform local security guards to keep an eye on the house.
    5. Inform your daily vender of newspaper, Milkman, and others about the duration of the vacations.

- *Final Preparations–* Check your travel documents before you leave home and keep them in a safe place where you'll be able to keep track of them easily- for example, a neck purse worn across your body rather than a pocket which they might fall out of or be stolen. Once you're at the airport, keep yourself busy: take an interesting book with you, walk around the duty-free shops or engage your mind by working through a book of crosswords or sudoku puzzles. You'll find that this will help you take your mind off any travel-related worries.

- ***Diet-related suggestions*** - Many experts on stress also suggest changing your diet slightly the day before you fly and while you're on your flight. On the day earlier to flying, avoid eating rich or fatty foods, and try not to drink too much tea, coffee or alcohol, after all, there's nothing worse than being hungover when you're flying high in the air!

The majority of travel-related stress, however, can be beaten simply by remaining calm and composed. Make sure you keep your head above water when traveling, and if adverse events do occur, simply tackle them one step at a time. As a result, you'll find that your holiday will get off to a much more relaxing start - a trend that can only continue throughout your vacation.

Problem No 45 - Traffic Jams Stress

Stress Builder- I Get Irritated And Highly Stressed, When Struck In The Traffic. How Can I Relax My Self In Those Conditions?

<u>Explanations</u> - This is the most common problem I believe we all face on a regular basis. The rapid developments in the automobile industry and driving to the long distances to our jobs have made this thing worse. Along with this, there is also our dependency on motor cars creating problems and stress in our every day lives.

Supportive plans to combat this stress-

- *<u>Adopt to the situations</u>*- There is an old saying –If you can't change your destiny, change your attitude; if you are stuck in the traffic, rather than getting irritated and stressed, try to adjust to the problems as neither there is any of your faults nor you are responsible for it.

- *<u>Try to Sing away the stress</u>*- If you find yourself becoming angry or anxious when you're stuck in a traffic jam, fasten out a tune loud and strong. Not only can singing help to offset stress-related brain activity, but it also helps to slow down your heart rate and control your breathing. As you sing your favorite tunes, feel yourself slowly relax. Try using a radio station that plays popular music without words to serve as your background music.

- *<u>Listen to an Audio Support</u>*- If you travel long on a regular basis, keep a few audio books in a compartment in your car. If you're stuck in traffic, you can always pull one out and get lost in a thrilling story. A little audio leisure activity never hurts when you're stuck in a frustrating traffic jam.

- *<u>Play a Mobile Game</u>*- Play an entertaining game using your game pad to pass the time while stuck in a traffic jam. A good game you love that you never knew that the traffic ever existed.

- *<u>Have A Snack-</u>* Keep a delicious snack stashed in your glove compartment that's reserved only for traffic jams. Make it so tasty that you actually forget the traffic jam problems. When traffic grinds to a halt, pull out your snack and slowly enjoy every last bite. You deserve it.

- *<u>Plan your journey early</u>*- If you face a regular traffic jams on your way, look out for an alternative course to your destination, or if not possible, start off earlier in the morning to avoid the traffic and the stress.

- ***Do some exercise*-** Waiting for the signal is a good thing to do some relaxing exercise and some stretching exercise. If possible, get out of the car and shake your body; this will give the positive effects of the waiting.
- ***Try to carpool*-** If you travel a long distance and you know many people around who go to the same place as you do, go for the carpool. It will not only save money but also save the environment and the fuel. The greatest benefit is that you will never get bored or stressed in the traffic jams.

Problem No 46 - Dealing With Road Rage

Stress Builder- How Can I Deal With The Road Rage?

<u>Explanations</u>- Road Rage is a serious and deadly type of stress one can face. The increasing pressure and jams on the roads have made this evil a very common thing to see. People burst into anger and most often behave like the most dreaded criminals, when faced with this situation. No one knows that when he might have this type of situation in his life. The only difference between you and a road rager is how you deal with the situation and the stress behind it.

To protect yourself, you have to get a hold of your emotions. The worst thing that you want to happen is to meet someone who is as angry as you, or possibly, even more possessed by rage. This will likely cause a confrontation on the road that may lead to an exchange of gestures, dangerous driving tactics and physical violence. If you are an innocent victim of road rage by some fuming driver, you must protect yourself.

Supportive plans to combat this stress-

- Don't retaliate. Never take the other driver personally; he/she is only reacting on a road rage instinct. Take the next right turn and choose an alternate route to your destination. If necessary, pull over and cool off before continuing on your way.

- Be polite and courteous, even when you are not at the mistake. Try to analyze the problem. If there is a minor dent, it will not cost you much than your health.

- Don't make eye contact with an angry driver. An angry look is all he/she needs to increase the level of rage. The best advice is to safely get away from an angry driver as quickly as possible.

- If you are harassed by another driver and being followed, do not go home. Go to the nearest police booth or call the helpline number for help.

- Never underestimate other drivers' capacity for confusion. He may put you in deep trouble if the situation gets out of hand.

- Reduce your driving stress by allowing enough time to get where you are going. Know the roads that are under construction and listen to weather reports that may cause traffic delays. Practice patience and keep your cool.

- Do not endanger yourself by trying to evade a road rager. Drive the speed limit and observe all traffic control devices.

- Remember that you cannot control the drivers around you, but you can control the way they affect your well-being. Be calm and drive safely.

- Remember to be respectful while driving. Treat other people the way you would want to be treated.
- To deal with the utmost trouble, have a pepper spray in the car. Sometimes, the conditions go out of hand, and it is no harm to protect yourself in spite of your cool and peaceful intentions for the other person on the road.

Problem No 47 - Car Break down stress

Stress Builder- My Car Broke Down In The Middle Of The Road, How Can I Deal With This Stress?

<u>Explanation-</u> This is type of problem, which can happen to anyone and at any time. No one can predict that when he will face this type of problem, whether he is driving a new car or an old car. Stranded in the middle of the road, one can easily get confused and stressed, as most often one really does not know what to do.

There is not a proper way to deal with this problem rather than to keep the mind cool and stress away.

Supportive plans to combat this stress-

- <u>*Keep your mind cool*</u>- Rather than getting irritated and angry, drink water (From your water bottle, which you always carry) and keep neutral for some minutes. An angry and disoriented mind can never find any easy solutions.

- <u>*Try to find the exact fault*</u> – Rather than keep perusing your problem, get out of the car and try to find the exact problem. Do not try to be an expert and dismantle several parts, as it may damage further your existing problems.

- <u>*Seek a safe space-*</u> If your car has been stranded in the middle of the road, your first priority is to push your car to a safe space as it may not cause trouble to the others on the road.

- <u>*Pass Information*</u>- Rather than cursing your destiny or the car, inform your office or the home about the problem. This will not only release your urgency stress but also give you a peaceful mind.

- <u>*Seek help*</u>- If the problem is too complex, do not feel guilty about seeking help from the helpline/Police Post or the other drivers on the road.

- <u>*Refresh yourself-*</u> While waiting for help, why do not refresh yourself to deal with the problem? Have snacks, energy drinks, or listen to music.

Problem No 48 - Seasonal Affective Stress Problems

Stress Builder- I Get Deeply Stressed When The Unpleasant Weather Affects My Work

Explanations- Imagine that a person woke up to the coldest morning of the season from his bed, and there is a strong possibility that he experiences a mild bout of stress and depression, which is commonly known as the winter blues. Experts claim that a spurt in the cases of depression during the winter months is quite common. It is known as the seasonal affective disorder (SAD), and it becomes worse during the cold and cloudy days of the winter.

With the drop in temperature, exposure to fog and decreased sunlight, the entire rhythm of the body begins to changes during the winter.

SAD affects half a million people every winter between September and April, peaking in December, January, and February. The "Winter Blues", a milder form of SAD, may affect even more people.

Related Facts about SAD-

- Studies show that three out of four **SAD s**ufferers are women.
- The main age of onset of SAD is between 18 and 30 years of age.
- SAD occurs in both the northern and southern hemispheres, but is extremely rare in those living within 30 degrees latitude of the equator
- The severity of SAD depends both on a person's vulnerability to the disorder and his or her geographical location

Symptoms-

- A diagnosis of SAD can be made after three consecutive winters of the following symptoms if they are also followed by complete remission of symptoms in the spring and summer months, which includes:

    1. Depression: misery, guilt, loss of self-esteem, hopelessness, despair, and apathy
    2. Anxiety: tension and inability to tolerate stress
    3. Mood changes: extremes of mood and, in some, periods of mania in spring and summer
    4. Sleep problems: desire to oversleep and difficulty staying awake or, sometimes, disturbed sleep and early morning waking

5. Lethargy: feeling of fatigue and inability to carry out normal routine.
6. Overeating: craving for starchy and sweet foods resulting in weight gain
7. Social problems: irritability and desire to avoid social contact
8. Sexual problems: loss of libido and decreased interest in physical contact

Causes

As sunlight gives its effects to the seasonal activities in humans, as seasons change, there is a shift in our "biological internal clocks" or circadian rhythm, which is partly due to these changes in sunlight patterns. This can cause our biological clocks to be out of "step" with our daily schedules. Melatonin, a sleep-related hormone secreted by the pineal gland in the brain, has been linked to SAD. This hormone, which may cause symptoms of depression, is produced at increased levels in the dark. It is also known as the Happy Hormone. It is also an antioxidant that can cross cell membranes easily and even fight several diseases. Therefore, when the days are shorter and darker, the production of this hormone increases.

Supportive plans to combat this stress

For mild symptoms, spending time outdoors during the day or arranging homes and workplaces to receive more sunlight may be helpful. One study found that an hour's walk in winter sunlight was as effective as two and a half hours under bright artificial light.

Try to get up at the same time every day; this will readjust your body clock.

- *Get outside*- Even a cloudy day can have twice as much as light than your office.
- *Morning walk*- Morning light is more effective than later day light.
- *Regular Exercise*- It can beat the blues away.
- *Holidays-* Plan out your winter vacations.
- *Self medications*- Caffeine and alcohol are not the solutions.Ttry to avoid them.
- *Fresh air*- Try to work near the fresh air.
- *Party* - Winter is the season to enjoy, so organize a party or social activities.

Problem No 49 - Stress In The BPO Sector

Stress Builder- What Kind Of Stress In The BPO Sector

Explanations- This is the gift of the modernization and the facilities we use regularly. The rapid growth has created more harm to the body on an emotional and physical level than a person living around 20-30 years ago. Call center/BPO has a high level of stress as related to other corporate offices. The main reasons behind this are described below-

Causes-

- ***Extended Working Hours-*** Long working hours is the greatest cause of stress for call center agents, just ahead of work timing. Long hours, in it, are a combination of workload, call volume and travel time. Since most BPO players are still mainly voice-based, the workload is inconceivable, and the time involved in traveling between home and office. The troubles of the operational heads are worse-they regularly clock 17-18 hours per day working their shift besides staying back for customer discussion calls.

- *Work Timing-* Many in the industry, in fact, feel that this is the root cause of most of the dissatisfaction trouble in all centers. It is indeed a great matter that the geographical time difference between the countries creates the additional stress by working in the odd hours.

- *Workload-* Having heavy work load and the desired targets to fulfill make the problems worse. Dealing with the international atmosphere of customers also gives stress to the unfamiliar workers.

- ***Repetitive Nature of Work-*** No surprises here- It is a commonly accepted fact that the monotony of the same kind of work in call centers can indeed be very stressful. The survey suggested that the male fresher seemed to be the group particularly affected. Again, solutions are not readily available, though measures like hiring retired personnel or housewives might be of some succor since these groups with more experience tend to get frustrated the least. Some others have also devised innovative measures, like periodic job rotation, though not much can be expected out of these in a pure call center environment.

- ***Insufficient Holidays****-* When the job is to deal according to international standards, there are no chances to adopt your own customs and traditions, which give the stress in the long run. Imagine all your family members are enjoying festivals at home, and you are working in your office dealing with customers from the another country.

- ***Pressure to Perform on Metrics-*** This is particularly galling for the first timers working in an environment where every single action needs to conform to a performance measuring metrics. This looks unlikely to go away soon since most call centers are keen on different standards certifications. This is an absolute business necessity for most companies to follow these quantifiable business metrics to attract customers and add stress levels to perform well in your jobs.

- ***Stress: Health Issues-*** As compared to the call center industry with coal miners, the call centers is an extremely harmful job. The call center related ailments are being treated separately in many places. People in senior managerial positions with five-plus years of experience are less affected by these illnesses because they maintain a more regular work schedule and timing.

- ***Travel Time-*** Most call centers are located on the outskirts of cities, and therefore, most employees spend a long time traveling to and from their offices. Traveling for a long duration in heavy traffic is the major cause of stress.

- ***Call Volume/Number of Calls-*** While the overall workload is quite high, call volume in itself is proving to be a major cause of stress. In most call centers, there is hardly any respite between two calls; not only is this disconcerting, but also, in the case of one abusive call immediately following another, it can be psychologically disturbing too. In addition, most agents accept these calls under an assumed identity: constantly maintaining a false image amidst an influx of calls afflicts all agents – both experienced ones as well as first-timers.

- ***Overtime-*** Though most companies encourage overtime with incentives, in particular the first timers, who, with the goal of making more money, eagerly do overtime, but once they are into it, the stress factor starts showing up. Overtime, in concert with long working hours and travel time, is turning out to be a potent combination, causing call center-related stresses.

- ***Sleeping Disorders-*** Dealing with international customers at odd hours creates severe ailment afflicting people working in call centers. Apparently, this affects first-timers more severely, as they take time to get used to their biological clocks, but even experienced people or managers are not able to completely escape from it. Some call centers are looking at devising innovative mechanisms like flexible shifts with sleeping arrangements in the office premises as possible solutions.

- ***Digestive System Related Disorders-*** Working long and odd hours without any sleep and eating food supplied by external caterers every day has caused a common suffering from digestive problems. Especially, for the large number of girls working in the industry, the problem is even more severe.

- ***Depression-*** Coping with growing mental fatigue and increasingly punishing physical environments, depression is the obvious end result. This is the most common and dangerous problem among call centers employees.

- ***Severe Stomach-Related Problems-*** Continuing digestive problems lead to severe stomach disorders like gastroenteritis; as doctors in major cities agree, in recent times, many of the patients with various stomach ailments are from call centers.

- ***Eyesight Problems***-Globally call center industry employees are considered a high-risk group for eye-related problems. While the quality of monitors might impact these disorders, sitting constantly without sufficient breaks seems to be the basic reason.
- ***Ear Problems***- Since a call center job involves taking calls throughout the shift, sitting with headphones and hearing for long durations certainly creates the ear and hearing problems. While the quality of headphones does make a difference, the problem is that hearing in high tone without much break is the main concern.

Supportive plans to combat this stress-
- ***Make friends at work-*** While doing stressful jobs, the more you share your time with your friends in the office, the more you feel relaxed. The friend circle not only shares your emotions but you can also release your stressful experiences with them.
- ***Spend time with your family-*** As the job expects you your odd timmings, try to share most of your time with your family members. You will get support from them, which is desperately needed.
- ***Go for relaxation exercises*** – As they are designed for instant relaxation –

Visual Concentration and Rhythmic Massage:
1. Open your eyes and stare at an object, or close your eyes and think of a peaceful, calm scene. With the palm of your hand, massage near the area of pain in a circular, firm manner. Avoid red, raw, swollen, or tender areas.
2. Inhale/Tense
3. Exhale/Relax
4. Breathe in (inhale) deeply. At the same time, tense your muscles or a group of muscles. For example, you can squeeze your eyes shut, frown, clench your teeth, make a fist, stiffen your arms and legs, or draw up your arms and legs as tightly as you can.
5. Hold your breath and keep your muscles tense for a second or two.
6. Let go! Breathe out (exhale) and let your body relax.

Slow Rhythmic Breathing
1. Stare at an object or close your eyes and concentrate on your breathing or on a scene.
2. Take a slow, deep breath and, as you breathe in, tense your muscles.
3. As you breathe out, relax your muscles and feel the tension draining.
4. Now, remain relaxed and begin breathing slowly and comfortably, concentrating on your breathing, taking about 9 to 12 breaths a minute. Do not breathe too deeply.

5. To maintain a slow, even rhythm as you breathe out, you can say silently to yourself, "In, one, two; out, one, two." It may be helpful at first if someone counts out loud for you. If you ever feel out of breath, take a deep breath and then continue the slow breathing exercise. Each time you breathe out, feel yourself relaxing and going limp. If some muscles are not relaxed, such as your shoulders, tense them as you breathe in and relax them as you breathe out. You need to do this only once or twice for each specific muscle group.

6. Continue slow, rhythmic breathing for a few seconds up to 10 minutes,

7. To end your slow rhythmic breathing, count silently and slowly from one to three.

8. Open your eyes. Say silently to yourself: "I feel alert and relaxed." Begin moving about slowly.

- **_Other relaxation methods_**- Music, Aromatherapies, and Chew gum in free time will reduce your stress level.

- **_Eat stylish-_** Do not load up on simple carbohydrates like sugar that will send your insulin surging. Have lots of vegetables, fruits and whole grains, and walk away from fatty meals, sodium, alcohol and caffeine

Problem No 50 - Mobile Lost Stress

Stress Builder- I Have Lost My New Mobile. I Am Deeply Depressed. What Should I Do?

Explanations- This is also the most common incident which happens to many of us too often. Losing a mobile, whether it is new or old, definitely gives stress to anyone, but rather than cursing the moment, stay calm in the easier way like-

Supportive plans to combat this stress

- **_Depression_**- Coping with the phone loss will certainly give depression when a lot of personal things like - songs, movies, and contact numbers are stored in it. The first moment is to inform the telephone operator about the loss so that they can stop the activations of the phone instantly. This will stop the misuse of your phone. Also, inform the Police about the loss; this will safe guard you from any problem related to the loss.

- **_Take a supportive Plan always_**- Nowadays, before saving any documents, movies, or contact numbers, try to have a back up or a copy of each and every detail on your computer or C.D. This will never let you stressed because of the data loss.

- **_Keep your mobile safe_**- I have seen most of the people holding their mobile carelessly in their hands, which is more likely to be lost. Always keep your phone in safe body pouches or handbags – Not in the pockets, as it can create health problems.

- **_Do not look behind_**- There is an old saying-

> **You can not change your past, but you can ruin your future by worrying about it today.**

Rather than stressing yourself, go out and purchase a new mobile with several new features; after all, this is a genuine idea to purchase a new handset, and enjoy yourself.

www.ingramcontent.com/pod-product-compliance
Lightning Source LLC
LaVergne TN
LVHW070530070526
838199LV00075B/6749